A KNIGHT AND HIS ARMOR

About the Author

Ewart Oakeshott was born in 1916. He began collecting swords while still in school at Dulwich, and has since built up a superb collection, specializing in the medieval period. His books include *The Archaeology of Weapons, European Weapons and Armour, The Sword in the Age of Chivalry,* and the acclaimed "Knight" series. He always brings to his books a wide and deep knowledge of his subject, and a witty and pithy style. The *Times Educational Supplement* rightly called him "one of those rarely gifted researchers who combine exhaustive investigation with absorbing enthusiasm." Oakeshott (and three friends) founded the Arms and Armour Society, a concern with a worldwide membership. His home is in Ely, close to Cambridge, England.

A KNIGHT
AND HIS ARMOR

Second Edition

EWART OAKESHOTT F.S.A.
Illustrated by the author

Dufour Editions

First published 1961,
this revised second edition published 1999

Published in the United States of America by
Dufour Editions Inc.,
Chester Springs, Pennsylvania 19425

ISBN 0-8023-1329-9

Library of Congress Cataloging-in-Publication Data

Oakeshott, R. Ewart.
  A knight and his armor / Ewart Oakeshott ; illustrated by the
author. – 2nd ed., rev.
    p. cm.
  Includes bibliographical references and index.
  ISBN 0-8023-1329-9
  1. Armor, Medieval.   I. Title.
U810.025 1999
623.4'41--dc21   99-26158
                                                        CIP

Printed and bound in the
United States of America

Contents

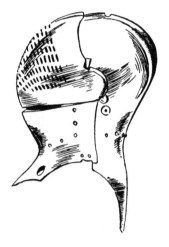

*Helm of Sir Giles Capel, made, possibly in London, 1511
(Metropolitan Museum, New York.) A type of helm developed from the
great bascinet which was popular in the early sixteenth century.*

TO MY GOD-DAUGHTER
JANE PERRY

Fig. 1a. Mark of the Guild of Nuremberg armorers.

The History of Armor

TO study medieval armor is to glimpse not just the look, but also the feel, the imagination, the tone, the horror, and the majesty of a past time. Armor provided protection, yes, but it also reflected the tenor of the times and the importance of its wearer, and it provides us with insightful stories of an era rich in legend and history.

A little more than 500 years ago, a knight of the ancient Franconian family of Schott had a splendid armor made for him by one of the celebrated armorers of Nuremberg. This knight, named Kunz Schott of Hellingen, died in 1526, but his armor survives in nearly mint condition. Complete, undented, brilliant, it is a remarkable work of craftsmanship.

It was made between 1490 and 1497, when Schott and forty other knights owned the great castle at Rothenburg. These 41 knights offered the services of a small professional army to the barons of Southern Germany to fight for hire in their endless private wars; altogether there would have been perhaps 500 well-trained, war-hardened fighting men, whose lair was this castle that still stands not far from the city of Nuremberg.

In 1497 Schott was elected by his fellow-knights to be commander of the force and fortress; one of his first acts was to start a fierce and bitter little war against Nuremberg in answer, so he said, to the irritating hostility shown to the Rothenburg knights by the City Council. Because of this war, we can establish within a year or two the date Schott's armor was made, which must have been completed before the war started. To build such an armor took a long time, and many visits had to be paid to the armorer for fittings. If Schott had shown his nose inside Nuremberg after he began his war in 1497, he would have lost it and his head in no time at all, even supposing that any armorer in the city's guild would have undertaken to work for a customer at war with the city. So we can assume the armor was made before the war began late in the 15th century. And, based on the style and fashion of the armor, we know it could not have been made earlier than 1490. We know, as well, that the armor was made in Nuremberg, for it bears the mark of the Nuremberg armorers' guild, a Gothic letter N surrounded by a pearled or dotted border (fig. 1a), which is stamped inside the breastplate. In addition, Schott's armor has certain peculiarities of form that are characteristic of Nuremberg workmanship.

Today this armor is polished bright, but when Schott wore it the surface would probably have had a black or dark purplish finish; his coat of arms, engraved on the top of the breastplate, would have been bright with the painted colors that have since worn away. The coat of arms and the crest no doubt stood out bravely against the dark background. Consisting of a shield of four squares colored alternately silver and red, the coat of arms bore the proper heraldic terms "Quarterly, Argent and Gules." The crest revealed a pair of buffalo horns, also Argent and Gules. (This armor is in a magnificent private collection in England, that of Mr. R T. Gwynn of Epsom.)

Schott's career as the leader of a free company seems to have been successful. Soon after his appointment he sent a letter of formal defiance to one of the great Princes of Germany, the Elector Palatine, who, Schott said, was withholding the property of Hornberg, which was Schott's by inheritance. We know nothing of what came of this affair, but Schott must have felt pretty confident to provoke so powerful a magnate. At some time during the early years of Schott's harrying of the Nurembergers, one of their councilors, Wilhelm Dering, had the bad luck to fall into his hands. Schott had him dragged up to Rothenburg, where his right hand was cut off. Dering was then sent back to the city with a rude message to the council. For this act the Emperor, Maximilian I, outlawed Schott, who doesn't seem to have been worried. Another great baron, the Markgraf (Count) Friedrich of Bayreuth, supported Schott, who carried on as before. All this time, of course, Schott's company of men would serve in the pay of any baron who wanted them. When money talks, mercenaries listen. Whenever there were no clients hiring his force, Schott would take his men out on their own account to pick up what loot they could find or steal.

Several years later Schott entered the service of the Markgraf Casimir of Brandenburg, as commander of the little town of Streitburg. Here Schott's activities caused a confederation of the barons of Swabia to send a note to the Markgraf warning him that, unless he put a stop to Schott's doings, they would devastate his lands. Casimir, as the story goes, had Schott beheaded secretly at Cadolzberg in 1523.

Since Nuremberg sympathizers put about this account of Schott's demise, we may take it with some reservation as to its complete accuracy; some evidence, for example, indicates that Schott was alive in 1525 and died of natural causes at Streitburg in 1526. We may safely conclude that the story of Schott's

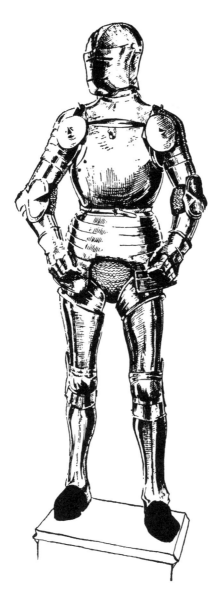

*Fig. 1. Armor of Kunz Schott von Hellingen.
Built in Nuremberg between 1490 and 1497.*

beheading, though dramatic, is not strictly true. The story may provide some truths as to Schott's reception among some people, encapsulating how despised he was in some circles. But the literal authenticity of the beheading strains credulity. Even so, whatever else Schott may have been, he was clearly a man of his time–fierce, aggressive, and unscrupulous. We must give him credit at least as a dashing captain and as a valiant, accomplished knight.

Figure 1 may give some idea of the shape and appearance of Schott's armor, but the drawing does little justice to the superb workmanship and form of the armor, which, in actuality, has a dark luster of steel and an alert, vigorous look. To see it up close, to sense the aliveness that still seems to be reflected in its grandeur, forces one to do a double-take in one's mind. For it is hard to believe that the warrior who wore this armor so often in battle, during both fall and siege, no longer fills it.

Schott's is not the only extant armor that is still complete; others like Schott's, made for historical personages, do survive. But many armors that you see in museums or private collections are composite, made from bits and pieces of similar armors–a leg from one, arms from another, breastplate from a third, and so on, perhaps finished with a helmet of a different period on top. Such an armor will probably have several modern restored pieces in it, too, but it will still hold much of the glamour we expect. Perhaps because of this glamour, and the romantic legends that tend to accompany it, many false impressions have been created and much nonsense has been written about armor, so let's clear up a few misconceptions right away.

To begin with, when armor was in everyday use, something familiar and lived with, it was never called "a suit of armor." It was simply called "an armor," or, more often, just "harness"; in fact, the expression "he died in harness" doesn't mean that a man who dies doing his job is like a horse: it goes back to the time of armor. The expression "suit of armor" was not used until about 1600.

Then there is the matter of "chain-mail." This expression, denoting a protective covering made of small inter-linked iron rings, has passed into the language, yet it is incorrect. What it refers to is simply "mail," flexible armor consisting of rings linked together. The Celts used mail as early as the fifth century BC; so did the Romans, who called it *macula,* which means a mesh or net.

The Norse people, the Vikings and their predecessors, oftentimes used various "net" expressions to describe mail. These people often spoke of their arms in poetic and roundabout terms: "his war-net, woven by cunning of smith," "bright were their byrnies, hard and hand-linked," "a bright breast-net," or "net of the spears." They never said a word about chains, always nets. If you look at a bit of mail, you'll see why. Its English name, mail, derives from the French, who took the Latin *macula* and turned it to *mailles*.

The most serious and stupid error is the old one about the weight of armor. Men never had to be hoisted into their saddles with cranes; the relative weight and composition of armor are widely known and appreciated, yet this piece of time-honored idiocy appears in book after book and film after film. Some extremely thorough tests, conducted thirty-odd years ago, should dispel the lingering misconceptions for anyone who cares about accuracy. The tests involved men wearing real armor, not light tin or aluminum stage armor. Some of the best of these tests were sponsored by the Metropolitan Museum in New York, and they were filmed. They show how easily a man armed in full plate can run, jump into the air, lie down on his front or his back and get up again without help, and also jump onto his horse and off again. Naturally, a man—even a very fit one—would soon get exhausted if he carried on in this way for long. Our ancestors were trained from an early age to wear armor and fight in it, but they didn't expect to have to walk or run in it; full armor was to be worn on horseback, where the horse carried the weight and supplied the power. Even so, a proper warrior was expected to be able to leap into his saddle, from ground level, without touching the stirrup, with his entire armor on. Edward I of England was well known for being able to do it (one suspects that he was rather fond of doing it, too), as was his better-known descendant Henry V.

Most of the armors in England dating before about 1550, even in the great national collections, are

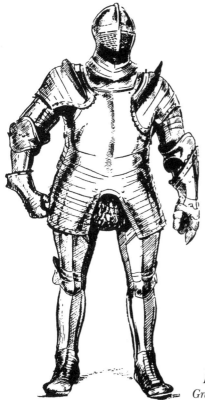

composite, but some survive that are as complete and well-preserved as Schott's. The armors of Henry VIII, for instance, both in the Tower of London and the magnificent one at Windsor Castle, are brilliant armors that have survived intact. The one at Windsor Castle stands on the stairs, and as you come up to it you can easily imagine stand-

Fig. 2. Armor of Henry VIII.
Built in the Royal Armories at
Greenwich, 1537 (Windsor Castle.)

ing and possibly quaking before that most royal personage himself (fig. 2). In the Tower of London, too, are several armors made in the royal workshops at Greenwich for well-remembered noblemen of the court of Elizabeth I, though all of these are late in date, not medieval. For complete armors of the period when armor was battle-dress, not court dress, we must go to the Continent. There are complete war-harnesses dating from about 1420 to 1550, armors splendid to look at, fresh and gleaming but dented and marked with the scars of war.

What we lack in surviving armors is more than made up by our wealth of tomb-effigies, sculptures, and paintings. The effigy of a knight on a tomb in white stone, laid out like a fish on a slab, looks terribly dead, though it is far from uninteresting; in nearly every case such an effigy will show an exact replica of the armor worn in life by the warrior who lies confined beneath it. The manuscript pictures often reproduced in history books of the Middle Ages may have a strange look about them, especially to an eye accustomed to photographs or pictures drawn with regard to the laws of perspective. But the best of them provide insights into the past, showing clearly how people dressed and lived and worked and fought. A thing to remember, though, is that not all medieval art conveys an accurate, compelling look at the past; most does, but not all. While good examples are instructive, bad ones are misleading.

Another thing to remember about medieval armor is that, until the fifteenth century, only vague differences in style existed among the nations of Europe. For this reason, if we want to find out how an English baron would have armed himself at, say, the battle of Lewes in 1264, the pictures in a Swedish or a Spanish manuscript would tell us what we want to know as well as the sculptures in a German or a French cathedral. After 1350, as we shall see later on, distinct national styles emerged, and they became more sharply defined as time went on.

It is tempting to think that only English monuments or pictures will do, but throughout the Middle Ages England was politically unimportant. France, Spain, and Germany were the big powers, and they, together with Italy, England, Denmark, Norway, Sweden and others, were part of a greater unit, Christendom; except for common materials, armor generally was not made in England until 1519, when Henry VIII brought over some German armorers and established his own royal workshops at Greenwich. Until then, there was no English-style armor. Until about 1420 all European armor was of an international pattern. By that date, distinctive Italian and German fashions had developed and men armed themselves according to the national styles they preferred.

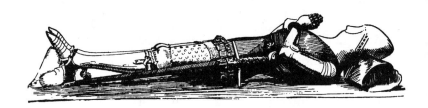

*Fig. 3. Effigy of Sir Reginald Cobham on his
tomb in the Church at Lingfield, Surrey. He was one of
the Black Prince's captains, and died in 1361.*

The Making of Mail and Plate

IN this book I am concerned with the armor of the later part of the Middle Ages, from about AD 1100 to 1500, so I will not look in detail at the armor of early people. The armor of the Greeks and Romans deserves its own study; it matters little if we neglect it here since Roman armor had practically no influence upon the development of European medieval armor, whereas the armor of the barbarians did: that is, the Gauls, Goths, Longobards, and Franks. The Gothic horsemen who overran Italy in the fifth and sixth centuries were armed in the same way as the knights of William of Normandy at Senlac, or like the Crusaders of the twelfth and thirteenth centuries, with only minor differences. Like their descendants, they rode heavy war-horses, fought with lance and broadsword, and wore helmets and mail shirts and

21

Fig. 4. Making mail. The tool in the craftsman's right hand automatically inserts and closes the rivets on each ring.

carried shields. They set the pattern of battle tactics and armament for a thousand years. Figures 5 and 6 show what a warrior looked like in a complete harness of mail in about 1250, and in full plate in about 1375. The period of mail extends to about 1350, and the period of plate is from about 1350 to 1650, though after 1550 its use was by no means general and its forms were becoming decadent.

There were armors made of other materials; an entry in an inventory of Charles VI of France, for instance, in 1411, is for a complete harness for man and horse made of Syrian leather, and we know that horn and whalebone were sometimes used.

Keep in mind that mail is a flexible fabric, very hard and not too heavy, strong enough to prevent most cutting blows from penetrating it, though somewhat vulnerable to the thrusts of spears. Though mail kept ordinary arrows out very well, it could not keep out crossbow bolts or the terrible arrows of the Welsh and English longbow. Mail is made from iron rings inter-linked so that each ring has four others linked

A few rings of mail,
showing how they are
interlinked.

Fig. 5. A complete mail harness of about 1250.

Fig. 6. A complete harness of plate of about 1360. This sort of
armor was used all over Europe between about 1350 and 1420.

through it. The rings are made from iron wire with the ends of each ring flattened, overlapped and riveted, or (up to the end of the fourteenth century) "solid" rings punched from a thin plate. Where these solid rings were used, they were arranged in alternate rows with the riveted ones.

Garments of mail—shirts, hoods, leggings, mittens—were made on the same principle used for knitted garments made of wool, by increasing or decreasing the number of stitches (rings) in a row, or the number of rows, according to the way the line of the garment went in or out. We know a good deal now about the making of mail, but nothing of how the patterns of the garments were recorded. Analysis of existing garments has shown clearly that they were made like other knitted items, so there can be little doubt that mail-makers used something like modern knitting patterns. "Solid" or "closed" rings were probably punched out of a thin sheet of metal, while "open" or "riveted" rings were made from wire. A length of wire would be wound around the diameter of a rod. This would produce a long coil, which would be cut up one side from end to end, resulting in a number of rings. These rings would be heated until they were softened a little; the two ends of each ring would be flattened and pierced ready for the rivets. Then the rings would go from the smith to the mail-maker, who would assemble them according to his pattern, making sure to rivet each one.

We still don't know much about the actual processes of plate armor-making, but we are learning a good deal from studying the few known illustrations of armorers at work, from lists of tools and from a close analytical study of the way mail-making methods were worked out. We know something, too, of the organization of armorers' workshops, though our knowledge in this area is tantalizingly little. Some evidence, for instance, suggests a great deal of specialization occurred among mail-makers. Some time between the years 1298 and 1344 an Italian writer, Galvano Fiarnma, produced a work called the *Chronichon Extravagans*, in which he describes something of the armorers' work in Milan, one of the most important centers of armor-making from the mid-thirteenth century until the sixteenth. "In our territory," Fiarnma writes, "are to be found immense numbers of work-men who make every manner of armor—hauberks, breast-plates, plates, helms, helmets, steel skull-caps, gorgets, gauntlets, greaves, cuisses, knee-pieces; and lances, javelins, swords and so on. And they are of hard iron, polished brighter than a mirror. And there are a hundred hauberk-makers alone, not to mention the innumerable work-men under them who make rings for mail with marvelous skill. There are shield- and buckler-makers too, and makers of arms in incredible numbers. This city supplies all the other cities in Italy and exports arms even to the Tartars and Saracens." Fiarnma provides us here with excellent first-hand evidence that a variety of craftsmen assigned to make different pieces of armor existed during the medieval period. He also supplies evidence that a lot of plate armor was worn in the first half of the fourteenth century.

From later records we learn even more. Consider the sixteenth-century lists of the armorers in Henry VIII's royal armories at Greenwich. We know from these lists a little more about the specialization that went on in the workshop: "Hammermen" forged the plates, "Millmen" polished them when they were shaped, "Locksmiths" finished them by fixing the hinges and fastenings, and other craftsmen saw that the whole armor was assembled properly and fitted with linings.

In the fifteenth-century shops at Milan we find the kind of specialization we associate with modern mass-production on the assembly line; craftsmen were employed who did nothing but make the same particular part of the complete harness. Indeed it seems unlikely that at any time one man ever made a complete armor, any more than one man ever makes a whole automobile.

Plate armor was made from billets of steel or steely iron; these were hammered into flat plates by hand or by water-driven tilt hammers. The plates were then cut into shapes suitable for various pieces, which were made by hammering the shaped plates over "formers" or stakes like those used by modern silversmiths. These were little anvils of the appropriate shapes, each mounted on a vertical bar which could be fitted into the armorer's workbench or into a large wooden block.

The metal seems to have been worked cold for the basic shaping of the plate, though it was probably annealed once or twice during the process, but some details, like turned-over edges, must have been done with heat. After the pieces had been shaped, the most difficult part came next: fitting all the pieces together. This step obviously was the most important, for if the various pieces did not fit properly and closely over or under each other, the primary purpose of the armor would be defeated: it wouldn't protect its wearer, it wouldn't work flexibly, and it would have dangerous gaps in it. Examine a fine armor and you will see how closely each part fits into its neighbor. When this piecing together of the parts was finished, the parts went to the millman for cleaning and polishing on a water-powered wheel. If it was to be decorated, the etcher or gilder would have it next, and when he was done with it the locksmith would fit all the hinges, buckles and straps. Finally the linings would be put in and the whole armor properly assembled.

In fine armors the thickness of the pieces varies, not only between different pieces but even within different parts of the same piece. A breastplate is not only thicker than a backplate (and a backplate thicker than a vambrace or a leg harness), but a breastplate is itself thicker in front than round at the sides; and the front parts of helmet-skulls are thicker than the back. The hardness of the surfaces has been found to vary, too, for the outside is far harder than the inside.

The hardness of armor baffles, for it is almost like glass; you can hardly scratch the surface of a good piece of armor with anything, yet it is not brittle like glass. Some sort of casehardening must have been used, though it is not known precisely how it was done. This hardness was important to plate armor in the most practical terms: it prevented a weapon from penetrating, for the smooth, hard, rounded, polished surfaces of armor were meant to make even the most powerful blow glance off. We read quite often in accounts of fights in the later part of the Hundred Years' War how even the English longbow arrows didn't penetrate the French warriors' plate armor, which had developed in order to keep the longbow at bay, even when shot at close range. The arrows just glanced off. Even so, we do hear of shattering blows from axe, hammer, or sword that broke through plate armor.

Most good armors bear the mark of the armorer–the individual, and the workshop. In some cases only the principal pieces were marked; in others every piece was, sometimes even every plate. Occasionally we find a personal owner's mark on the outside, though more often such marks were scratched or painted on the inside (these marks include charms and good-luck signs). Schott von Hellingen's armor, for example, has the cross of Jerusalem painted in red on the inside of the fanplate of each poleyn (armor covering the knee) and inside each pauldron (armor covering the shoulder). His shield of arms is engraved on the outside of the top of his breastplate (fig. 59). These armorers' marks, a kind of signature, show how much pride was taken in the making of armor, that the armorer wanted to leave some sign that the craftsmanship was his, or that his allegiance leaned a certain way. In the making of armor we also see a kind of civic pride, for, in addition to armorers' marks, we sometimes find the "view mark" of the town in which the piece was made, or we see marks of particular governments (especially for armor made late in the medieval period).

Armor was never as heavy as is sometimes imagined. A full plate harness of about 1470 was no heavier–and sometimes was lighter–than the full marching kit of a World War I infantryman. The average weight of such armor was about 57 pounds, but keep in mind that this weight did not descend from the shoulders like a foot soldiers' outfit: instead, the weight of armor was distributed all over the wearer's body. And, contrary to popular notions, armor was fitted so that it was easy to wear. The greatest care was taken to get an exact fit; only a first-class tailoring job would do. Whenever possible, the customer was measured and fitted with each piece by the master-armorer. If the wearer wasn't available to be measured by the armor-maker, then exact measurements would be sent to the armor shop. In England or Spain, for example, armor would often be ordered from Milan or Augsburg. Sometimes measurements would be sent with garments made to fit, sometimes with wax models of the customer's limbs. Consider, for example, a duke of Touraine, who, in 1386, had "a little doublet made to be sent to Germany as a model for a pair of plates (breast and backplates) to be made for his person." Consider, as well, an entry in the accounts of the Royal House of Spain in the second quarter of the sixteenth century: "For wax for making a model of His Majesty's legs, to be sent to Mr. Desiderius Colman for the armor he is engaged on...." This care and concern for exact fittings applies to mail as well as to plate, though the flexibility of mail made the need for a great fit not as vital as with plate. Finally, anyone expecting to be a warrior began training to wear armor when he was seven years old, so by the time knighthood was bestowed on a warrior, he became accustomed to wearing armor. (The warrior class applied to any boy of noble birth as well as many others).

Noble medieval youths were trained to wear armor much as modern youngsters are taught to read and write: that is, they are schooled early on in the art. Juan Quejada de Reago, a knightly person writing early in the sixteenth century, said it was "necessary to begin the training of a man-at-arms as a child is taught to read by learning the A.B.C. (*Doctrina Della Arte Della Cavalleria*)." Every day the warrior-in-training wore armor and exercised in it, and when he was a man he would wear it for long periods and probably do a good deal of warring in it (in the Middle Ages, manhood generally commenced when the warrior was about fourteen years old). He was not only brought up to wear armor himself but was the proud inheritor of a tradition that his ancestors began a thousand years earlier: living most of their lives wearing armor.

Of course, armor did have some disadvantages. The greatest drawback was that, no matter how accustomed one got to wearing armor, even the most well-tailored suit could be stuffy and heat-retaining. A warrior could get fearfully hot inside his armor. Shakespeare apparently understood the problem, for

in his history play *The Second Part of Henry the Fourth,*
he has Prince Henry speak of kingship as

> Like a rich armor worn in heat of day,
> That scald'st with safety. (IV.v.30-31)

At the great battle of Agincourt in 1415, King
Henry V's uncle, the duke of York, a stout, middle-
aged man, died of exhaustion and heatstroke in his
armor.

Fig. 7.

How Armor Developed

EUROPEAN armor developed from its prehistoric beginnings along two separate streams, the "classical" and the "barbarian." The first was the bronze and iron armor of Mycenaeans, Greeks and Romans, which began in about 2000 BC and ended early in the Middle Ages in the East Roman (Byzantine) Empire. The second was the leather and mail armor of the barbarian Celtic and Teutonic peoples who fought for centuries against Rome before finally overthrowing that great empire in the fifth and sixth centuries. This armor endured in Europe until the seventeenth century.

In the last chapter I said that the Crusader of the twelfth century was armed in the same way as his Gothic ancestor of the fourth; well, the armor of a Gaulish warrior of 400 BC was the same in essentials as that of a Crusader. The basis of all European armors was the shirt of mail. The origins of mail are not known, but enough datable material has been found to show that the Celts used it as early as the fourth century BC.

Before mail, the barbarian warrior probably protected his body with a coat of leather, such as the "Buff Coat" so universally worn in the armies of Europe during the period 1650-1750, after armor had been finally discarded. Conical bronze hel-

Fig. 8. A Gallo-Roman statue of a Gaulish warrior of about 100 B.C., from Vachères.

mets and parts of large wooden shields have been found in graves dated as early as 700 BC. The Gauls who fought against Rome have left plenty of archaeological evidence of their armor: mail shirts, complete shields, many types of helmets, countless spears, and numerous swords. Knowledge of these things is filled in by Roman writers who described them in detail and tell us much about the fighting methods of their wearers. Several pieces of sculpture, large and small, have survived to complete the picture (fig. 8). It is a picture

Fig. 9. A mounted warrior of the ninth century. Redrawn from an embossed golden jug, found at Nagyszentmyklos in Hungary.

that would have held well in essentials for European warriors up to the time of the Normans in 1066. There are many illustrations of the first thousand years of our era showing this Gaulish influence clearly. For instance, Figure 9 is a mounted warrior embossed on the side of a great golden vase that was made in about AD 860. This vase is part of a treasure found at a place with a name English speakers find tough to pronounce, Nagyszentmyklos, in Hungary. I have redrawn the figure in a modern manner, for though the ninth century goldsmith showed the warrior's entire armor in careful detail, this warrior had a rather odd look and a very odd horse. He had no sword either; there was probably a good reason why he was shown without one, but for our purpose I have given him one. As you can see, his armor is like that of the Gaul from Vacheres (fig. 8) and even more like the Norman knights from the Bayeux Tapestry.

The mail shirt (called by the Nordic folk a "byrnie" and by the rest of Europe a "hauberk") was a long garment reaching almost to the knee. The neck opening was closed by a lace or a buckle and strap, and after about 1100 the short, loose sleeves became long and close-fitting. After 1175 the sleeves of many hauberks were finished off with mittens (generally known as "mufflers") that slipped over the hand. The muffler was a little bag of mail with a separate stall for the thumb; the palm of the hand was not, for obvious reasons, covered by the mail but by some sort of fabric sewn to the edges of the bag. This fabric had a slit in it so that the hand could be slipped out easily, for the muffler would only be worn when fighting was imminent. Until about 1250 an integral part of a complete hauberk was the mail hood. After 1250 the hood ("coif") was made as a separate garment. It was drawn over the head, and the face opening was closed and tightened by a flap fixed with a buckle or a lace (fig. 5). When it was on, it looked like a woolen Balaclava helmet.

Fig. 10. "Muffler" (mail glove) from the figure on the brass of Sir Robert de Septvans, at chartham Church in Kent (1306.)

In the earlier part of the period of mail, the legs were protected only by leather or linen trousers (cut tightly like jeans), which were often cross-gartered to the knee unless knee-length leather boots were worn, but after 1100 a well-equipped man-at-arms wore long stockings of mail that extended to and covered the feet. Held up by straps fixed to a belt around the waist, these stockings were called "chausses" (fig. 11).

This armor protected its wearer from the worst effects of most blows, but, since it was so flexible, it could not prevent the flesh it covered from being bruised or crushed. So under this armor the warrior

Fig. 11. Arming in mail. The man on the left is fastening his "chausses;" the one in the middle pulls on the "gamboised chishes" which cover his thighs, while the one on the right puts on his "hauberk" over the quilted and padded "gambeson."

wore clothes of leather—long "hose" on the legs and a close-fitting jerkin and a well-stuffed padded shirt (called variously an "aketon" or "gambeson"); these leather clothes were somewhat effective as shock-absorbers, but the warrior's first line of defense was always his shield or his agility. It was far better to dodge a blow altogether than to depend fully upon your outfit's ability to protect you.

Until about 1190 the hauberk was worn outside everything else, but after that time it usually was covered with a long flowing garment made like a nightshirt (figs. 7 and 12). This covering possibly served to keep rain off the mail, or to shade it from the heat of the sun, and at a later period to afford a field for the display of heraldic bearings.

The mail coif was worn over a small close-fitting padded cap like a hairnet, and over the coif was worn a small helmet. Until about 1050 or 1100 this nut-shaped cap is the one often associated in our minds with the Normans, though it had been in use in Europe from the early Iron Age (about 800 BC) and was popular in the early Middle Ages from Persia to Sweden. The prehistoric caps were made of thin sheets of bronze, but the early medieval ones were made of several triangular iron plates riveted onto a framework of bronze. The medieval caps had a horizontal band around the brow to which were fixed two or more curved bands meeting at the apex. After

Fig. 12. Mailed man-at-arms versus halberdier. This is the earliest form of the halberd as it was used early in the fourteenth century. The man wielding it wears an iron "kettle-hat," leather coif and padded gambeson.

1050 more and more of these helmets seem to have been made from a single plate of iron. And why would that be? Probably because the single plate of iron created an efficient, seamless defense. After 1150, a tall, flat-topped, straight-sided helmet that looked a bit like a saucepan emerged. But by about 1220, that pan-like helmet was replaced by a far more practical, close-fitting skull-cap: made of steel, this skull-cap prevailed along with the nut-shaped helmet.

What we have just canvassed was the basic harness of European warriors from 1050 to 1300. It was effective in that it could save the warrior from being killed by a battle blow, but it could not prevent injury, and in many cases the injury crippled; and when a warrior was shot at by longbowmen, the harness provided no defense at all because the narrow "piles" (arrow-heads) of the yard-long arrows, driven with tremendous force, went straight through the rings.

The words and work of Gerald of Wales should prove instructive. Known as Giraldus Cambrensis, a twelfth-century chronicler who, for all intents and purposes, was a medieval journalist, Gerald reported among other things upon a lot of the fighting on the Welsh borders in the late twelfth century. Describing a skirmish between the men of one of the English barons, William de Braose, and the Welsh, Gerald tells how a Welsh longbowman shot at a man-at-arms. The arrow pierced the man-at-arms in the thigh, going straight through his mail hauberk, mail chausses and leather hose, right through his leg, through the leather and mail on the inside and on through the wood and leather of his saddle into the horse. Against a weapon that could penetrate so well, creating physical damage and lots of worry and wonder, mail was obviously no use. Early in the fourteenth century, the effectiveness of the longbow against mailed men was shown with terrible clarity. That's when English yeomen trained to use the Welsh bow practically wiped out two Scottish armies at Dupplin (1332) and Halidon Hill (1333). Then, in 1346, an English army consisting of two-thirds longbowmen mowed down the proud chivalry of France at Crecy. And with that impressive display of firepower, the fearful fame of the longbow was carried through all of Europe. It was obvious to most military men that a defensive covering more effective than mail had to be devised. But what, pray tell, could counter the deadly effect of an accurate, penetrating arrow shot with rapid force by a skillful longbowman? And to think, the longbow was not the only defensive worry a warrior faced. For another infantry weapon appeared on European battlefields at this time, a great broad-bladed axe with a stout spike at its end like a spear. Mounted on a five-foot haft, this axe-like weapon later became known as the halberd. In a battle at Courtrai in Flanders (1302), the halberd was wielded by burly Flemish townsmen who wiped out a large and splendidly equipped force of French knights. Then, in 1315, a force of Swiss peasants unleashed the halberd with such deadly force that they cut an army of Austrian men-at-arms to pieces at Morgarten with it. In England, too, a dose of similar medicine was dished out when Robert the Bruce's army of Scots wrecked King Edward II's great army at Bannockburn in 1314. The weapons used in those battles amounted to an unchivalrous show of power, precision, and force that made mincemeat of the mailed man-at-arms, cutting cleanly and devastatingly through armor.

These events and these weapons no doubt expedited the development of plate armor, but they did not cause it. For many years—at least the first thirty years of the fourteenth century—experiments were carried out with various kinds of plate armor for the limbs. Keep in mind, as well, that solid defenses for the body had been in use for a long time.

In the middle of the thirteenth century hard defenses for the knees were added to the chausses. They were called "poleyns" and were fixed to the bottom of trouser-like coverings for the thighs made of stout padded material. Some of these "gamboised cuishes," as they were called, were made separately,

Fig. 13. Demy-greaves, about 1310

but some were made like a pair of breeches. Occasionally, after about 1230, the fronts of the shins were protected by light metal greaves (generally known as "demigreaves"), but those were rare until the end of the century. After about 1300 "closed greaves" came more and more into use. They were made of two plates, one for the front of the leg and one for the back, hinged together on the outside and fastened by straps and buckles on the inside (figs. 13 and 14).

Solid iron or leather defenses for the body came into use at the same time as demigreaves. No actual specimens survive of these defenses, which were worn under the surcoat, and it is only from what we can see in statues and pictures that we are able to guess at their shape. We have good literary evidence that plates of iron

Fig. 14. Closed Greaves, about 1325. Though closed greaves were more common after 1320, there is still evidence that they were worn as early as 1310.

were used as breastplates as early as 1190 (see Giraldus Cambrensis, *Topographia Hibernica et Expugnatio Hibernica, lib.*I, cap. xx; Guillaume le Breton, *Phillipide lib.*III, lines 494-8.) A more common type of defense developed; it was a called a "coat of plates," which is just what it was, a sleeveless coat made of many small overlapping iron plates fastened into a textile covering. Sometimes this covering was the surcoat itself; the plates were sewn or riveted inside the chest and back, leaving the flowing skirts free. In other types an entire coat of plates was made as a separate garment worn over the hauberk and under the surcoat (fig. 15).

This sort of reinforced mail was in general use among up-to-date and well-to-do men at arms until about 1340. But it was this sort of armor that was so vulnerable to the halberd and the longbow. Why? Because it was a defense with seams, which could be pierced, widened, pen-

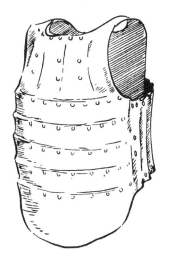

Fig. 15. A coat of plates. Small overlapping plate of iron riveted to the inside of a sort of sleeveless waistcoat. The side pieces wrap round the back where they are fastened by a buckle and straps, while the unarmored part of the coat with the neck opening in it goes over the shoulders and is tied to the side pieces by a "point."

etrated. It relied upon a series of layers–leather jerkin, padded aketon, hauberk of mail, coat of plates, surcoat–and it was getting awfully cumbersome. Soon what was cumbersome became ineffective, and so it had to go. The result was the complete harness of close-fitting flexibly jointed plate, which brought back the figure-hugging fit of the old style of simple mail, with the added benefit of a hard impervious surface.

The "coat of plates" was the principal defense for the body all through the fourteenth century, though after 1350 breastplates also were worn; these breastplates were made from a single plate, and often had a backplate to go with them. Evidence for this design and makeup comes mostly from sculptured figures, but in Munich there is an actual breast defense of just this kind, made in about 1390 (see figure 16). This defense covers the body from neck to waist, and, like the old-style coats of plates, it is covered with fabric (red velvet over canvas). This fabric extends downwards below the waist in a short skirt to the

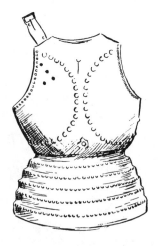

Fig. 16. Breastplate of the late fourteenth century (bayerisches National Museeum, Munich.)

inside of which are riveted five half-hoops of iron overlapping upwards. This defense for the abdomen is made in the old coat-of-plates manner, but it is more effective because the hoops extend around the sides instead of covering only the front. It was called the "fauld," and it became a constant feature as long as armor was worn.

Many complete cuirasses survive, all dating after about 1420. They show the accuracy of the medieval sculptors and painters who depicted armor, weaponry, and clothing. "Cuirass," by the way, means the whole armor for the body, breast, and back; the term came into use in the fifteenth century and developed from the thirteenth century "cuirie" or "cuiret," which meant a breast defense of (originally) leather. Another term for the breast and back, used from the fourteenth century onward, was "a pair of plates."

The leg harness (or "jamb") consisted of closed greaves, poleyns and "cuishes." The greaves (as shown in fig. 14) enclosed the whole lower leg; the poleyn was made of a single plate hollowed to enclose the knee-can and extended on the outside of the leg into a small flat plate, to protect the side and back of the knee. The main plate of the poleyn was fixed at top and bottom to narrow plates (called "lames"), one to fix it to the greave and the other to the cuish. The inside of the knee was unarmored, for it was needed to grip the saddle. The cuish was made

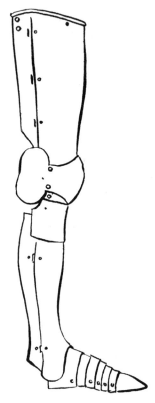

Fig. 17. Leg harness, about 1380. This is part of an armor (preserved in Chartres) which was made for king Charles VI of France when he was a boy.

of a single plate shaped to enclose the outside of the thigh.

After about 1380, a second, narrower plate was fastened to the main plate to extend it farther around the back of the thigh (fig. 17). The foot was armored as well; the "sabaton," which covered the feet, was made of a number of overlapping plates (they looked like the body of a wasp or of a lobster). The sabaton sometimes was fixed to the bottom of the greave and sometimes made as a separate shoe. When it was fixed to the greave, a couple of straps passing under the sole of the shoe held it in place, and when it was separate the plates were fixed to the shoe itself. The cuish would be held to the leg by straps passing around the thigh. A lace attached to a leather tag that was riveted to the top of the cuish would be braced up to a belt, much as the earlier mail chausses were suspended.

48

Armor for the arms was called the "vambrace"; this word, once applied only to forearm defense, was by the late fourteenth century applied to defense for the whole arm. The vambrace con-

Fig. 18. Vambraces, about 1360.

sisted of a "lower cannon," a small pair of plates enclosing the forearm in the same way that the greave enclosed the calf. This "lower cannon" was fixed to a "couter," a plate made like the poleyn to cover the elbow, which in turn was fastened to the "upper cannon," a pair of plates enclosing the upper arm. Unlike the cuish, the vambrace covered the entire circumference of the arm. The shoulder was protected by a series of small overlapping plates (called a "spaudler"). Though an unarmored spot was left where the arm joined the shoulder, a mail hauberk was still generally worn under the plate, thus leaving this gap not completely open. Even so, a small steel disc, called a "besagew," covered the weakness in this defense. The besagew had a strap riveted to its back that could be fastened to the spaudler so that the besagew hung free over the gap.

Armored gauntlets protected the hands; as early

Fig. 19. "Hour-glass" gauntlet, about 1360.

as the mid-thirteenth century small iron or whalebone or horn plates had been fixed to leather gloves, but by 1350 a simpler style had developed. A single plate shaped like an hourglass formed a short flaring cuff and a protection for the back of the hand and the side of the thumb. This plate was attached to a leather glove, to the fingers of which were riveted small overlapping plates (fig. 19). Many such gauntlets are shown on tomb effigies, and an almost complete pair, once belonging to Edward the Black Prince, is preserved in Canterbury Cathedral. These still have their leather gloves.

Helmets worn with armor of this style still had something in common with the old conical Norman helmet, but were taller and the sides and back descended lower. Instead of being worn on top of the mail coif, a deep curtain of mail was hung from its lower edges, covering the chin and neck and falling like a small cape over the shoulders (fig. 21). The English called this covering "aventail" whereas the French called it "camail." Various types of visors covered the face opening of these "bascinet" helmets. Some had a simple nose-cover, like the old Norman one, but instead of projecting downwards from the brow of the helmet, and being a permanent part of it, the fourteenth-century nose-cover was fixed to the front of the aventail; when not needed, this nose-cover hung down on the chest. When fighting was imminent, the warrior simply lifted the nose-cover over his nose and fixed it into a fitting on the brow of the helmet. As a result, the mail of the aventail was pulled up high to cover mouth and cheeks. It seems to have been a popular fitting, though it could not have been very effective. A much better visor was made from a larger plate covering the whole of the face opening. It was hinged to the brow, but like the smaller one could be taken off when no fighting was to be done. Many of these visors survive; some have simple shapes (fig. 20), but others have long pointed snouts. Above the snout are the eye-slits protected by projecting rims; below the snout is a similar slit, like a mouth, making the whole piece

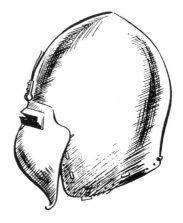

Fig. 20. Bascinet with hinged visor, called a "klappvisier" (Valeria Museum, Sitten.)

Fig. 21. Visored bascinet, about 1390 (armory of the castle of Churburg in the Tyrol.)

look like a grotesque face. Larger versions of this snouted visor also were devised. The sides were carried back, overlapping the front edges of the helmet. The sides were then attached to a pivot fixed to each side of the skull above the ears (fig. 21). These attachments are like hinges with removable pins: when a warrior did not need the visor, he simply pulled the pins out of the hinges. The pins were fixed to the helmet-skull with little chains so that they wouldn't get lost. When not fighting, the warrior took the visor off and carried it separately (or more probably gave it to his squire to look after).

Until about 1420 the body armor was still covered by a form of surcoat. No longer the flowing nightshirt-like robe of the thirteenth century, the surcoat was now a neat, closely fitting garment a bit like a sailor's shirt, fitting closely to the elegantly waisted "plates" beneath it. These coats (called today "jupon" or "gipoun" after the fashionable civilian garment

Fig. 22. Silver statuette of St. George, about 1430 (Barcelona.)

that it resembled) were usually richly decorated with the arms of their wearers. In England this garment was called a "coat of arms"–the origin of the modern expression denoting armorial bearings. After about 1420 (and even earlier on the Continent), this coat of arms was dispensed with, and the knight appears for the first time in his long history clad from head to foot in shining steel. In its own day, uncovered armor was called "white" or "alwyte" armor.

After about 1420 several important developments occurred in the style and design of armor.

Perhaps the most noticeable was the abandonment of the jupon, though by the late 1450s a similar coat of arms (now worn hanging loosely and called a tabard) came into fashion. Another was the prominence of the fauld. Figure 22 shows this prominence: the figure I have drawn here to illustrate a common style of armor of about 1430 is a silver statuette of St. George, in Barcelona. Made in the second half of the fifteenth century, it shows a Milanese armor in most faithful and accurate detail. I have taken few liberties in drawing this armor, though I have removed a shield that was added, possibly in the eighteenth century, and I have restored the tassets (small plates hanging

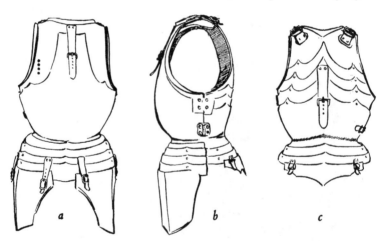

Fig. 23. Milanese cuirass of about 1460 from the front, side, and back. The four holes on the right side of the breastplate are to take the bolts fastening a removable lance-rest.

from the bottom edge of the fauld) to their correct position. At some time they were taken off and put back on their wrong sides. A similar armor is on the effigy of William Philipp, Lord Berdolf, in Dennington church in Suffolk. A series of hoops similar to the fauld was fitted to the lower edge of the waist of the backplate; this piece was called the "culet." Sometimes a loose plate was fixed to its lowest edge, a sort of rump-guard called a "hind tasset." By about 1450 the style of the fauld had changed; first the lowest plate was cut away in an arch in the middle; soon this arch increased in size until the lower plate divided into two, forming a pair of large tassets. Compare Figure 23, which shows a complete cuirass of this type (Milanese, of about 1460), with Figure 22.

In the St. George figure, you can see a small extra plate at the bottom of the breastplate, fastened in the center by a strap–a reinforcing piece called a "plackart"; as the century went on, this piece became larger. In the cuirass in Figure 23 it reaches nearly to the top of the plate. The backplate is made from several overlapping plates that give it a good deal of flexibility, for the holes in which the rivets work are in fact slots that allow a certain amount of up-and-down play to the plates. Figure 23b shows the cuirass from the left side; as you can see, breast and back-plates are hinged together on the left. To put the thing on, a warrior opened it out on its hinges, put it around his body and closed it. He then fastened the two pieces together at the right side with a stout strap on the breastplate that goes through a buckle on the backplate. The edges of the fauld and culet plates simply overlapped at the sides. You should notice in all these armors an important dimension of the overlapping plates: wherever possible, they always overlap away from the direction of potential thrusts and cuts of opposing weapons. It's an obvious point of craftsmanship, grounded in a practical, sensible concern for safety, which, after all, is the bottom line when it comes to armor. But it is astonishing how many imitation armors disregard this practical aspect.

Armor of this period had strong, turned-over edges in its principal plates, especially the edges of the armholes and the neck of breastplates. Similar stout ribs ("stop ribs" or "lisieres d'arret") were added to the top of cuishes; their purpose was to catch or turn aside the point of any weapon that ran along the plate. Even more noticeable is the way these stop ribs became exaggerated on the pauldrons, developing by 1450 into upstanding guards, protecting the weak spot where the helmet and breastplate met.

The actual forms of the armor changed little and varied hardly at all over the whole of Europe until about 1420, when two distinct national styles began to emerge, one in Italy and the other in Germany. The Italian style closely followed the earlier "International" style, though it tended to become heavier and more robust in appearance, and the small side-extensions (fan-plates) at the sides of poleyns and couters became larger and had a V-shaped dent in the middle. This dent carried the protection of the metal a little farther around to the back of the knee and into the bend of the elbow. By 1440 a great deal of the back of the knee and the bend of the elbow were covered. The little spaudler of the fourteenth century was often retained, but it was covered by a pauldron, a separate and complicated piece of armor made of several plates that protected the shoulder-blades better (fig. 24). In Italy these pauldrons became enormous at the back, but in many cases at the front each had a different shape. The right pauldron was cut away to keep it from interfering with the lance, which was often tucked under the arm when charging. The left pauldron became larger and covered most of the upper part of the breastplate, for it

Fig. 24. Vambraces, about 1460. Compare these with the ones shown in fig. 18.

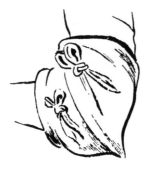

Fig. 25. Arming-point on a
Couter of about 1460.

served in place of the shield
that had largely gone out of
use by 1400. Similarly, extra
reinforcing pieces were
devised to cover the left
couter and to extend the left
pauldron. They couldn't be
used on the right arm, for
they held the arm in a bent
position. The left arm, pro-
vided you were fighting on horseback, remained fairly still. If you fought on foot you would not bolt these
extra "shield" pieces onto your
couter and pauldron, since you
wanted both arms to be free to
wield your sword with two hands
or to fight with a long poll-axe, a
very popular knightly weapon in
the fifteenth century (fig. 26).
Sometimes these reinforcing pauldrons and couters were fastened by
a pin pushed through a ring, but
more often "arming points" were
used—laces made of waxed twine,
sewn to the under-garments; the
ends were pushed through holes in
the plate and tied (fig. 25).

Like the Italian style of armor,

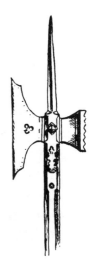

Fig. 26. A pole-axe
(Wallace Collection,
London.)

the German fashion began to emerge after 1420, its first sign being a development of the lower part of the breastplate with a rectangular box-like shape that the Germans called "Kastenburst" (See fig. 34a). A little later sprays of radiating embossed ridges were added; after about 1440 German armorers abandoned the box-shape and produced an elegant, slender armor whose breastplate was often decorated with these radiating ridges. Later, after about 1455, the Germans added the ridges of the rest of the armor–pauldrons, vambraces cuishes and poleyns, though never to the greaves. This German armor of the late fifteenth century has come to be called "Gothic" armor, probably because its long, slender forms and the delicate "tracery" of its decoration give it a sort of superficial resemblance to Gothic architecture. Some of the sharpest-looking, most beautiful armors are of this kind. Some splendid ones in Vienna are extremely handsome examples of superb craftsmanship, but they were not really meant for fighting; they were "full-dress" armors. In the fifteenth century, armor had a social function, symbolizing wealth and status, with certain kinds being worn for special occasions. For actual warfare, simpler (and for that reason often more beautiful) harnesses were made. Called "field armors" or "hosting harnesses," they were usually plain and undecorated. The armor of Schott of Hellingen is a good example.

Even so, many of the finer ones were embellished with sprays of embossed ridges and flutings. These were not just to make the armor pretty; on thin plates they performed the same stiffening function as the ridges in corrugated iron, thus shoring up the defense (fig. 27).

At the close of the fifteenth century the German and Italian styles merged, producing a type of armor that has come to be known as "Maximilian" because it covers the period of that romantic and knightly, but most unstates-manlike individual's reign as emperor (1493-1519). This armor is rounded and burly in form; we can refer to Schott's armor as an early example. Some of this armor is closely covered in every part (except the greaves) with closely set flutings, which tended to run parallel with each other, not to fan out in sprays as in the earlier Gothic style. In its time this ridged and fluted armor was known as "crested" armor. Toward the end of the fifteenth century a new piece was added to the harness. After about 1490 the breastplate became shorter, reaching at the top only to the upper part of the breastbone instead of to the neck, so a close-fitting protection for the throat and upper chest, called a "gorget," was worn with it. The gorget generally took the form of a high collar made of three or four narrow horizontal lames reaching up to the jawbone. Later I will describe how it was worn.

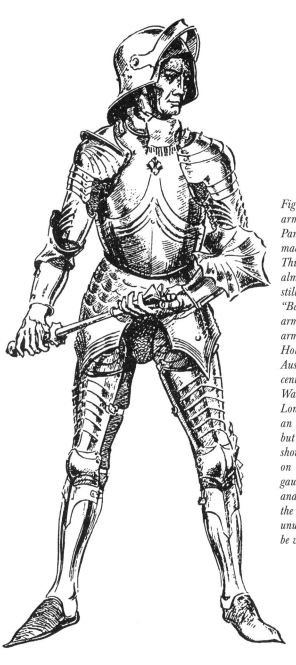

Fig. 27. "Gothic" field armor of Freiherr Pancraz von Freyberg, made in about 1475. This harness, which is almost complete and still has its matching "Bard" or horse armor, came from the armory of the castle of Hohenaschau in Austria. It is magnificently displayed in the Wallace Collection in London, mounted on an armored destrier, but lack of space I have shown it being worn on foot, without gauntlets or sabatons and with no bevor over the chin. It was not unusual for armor to be worn like this.

Fig. 28. Gauntlets.

a. From Churburg,
about 1390.

b. From Churburg, about
1425 (German style.)

c. Milanese, about 1460.

d. Gothic, about
1470.

e. "Maximilian" style,
about 1520..

The short, single-plate gauntlet with the flaring cuff and the small plates fixed to the fingers of leather gloves was used until the second quarter of the fifteenth century, when larger and more complex designs came into use. The drawings show more clearly than words how these fifteenth-century gauntlets developed (fig. 29).

A considerable variety of helmets was worn during the fifteenth century; most of them had developed by about 1440 and their styles changed only in minor respects until after 1500. Up to about 1425 the tall, snout-visored bascinet was the most popular, though at the beginning of the century solid plates had in some cases begun to be used in place of the mail aventail. These solid plates were distinguished from others by their names: they were called "great bascinets." These began to change form after 1425. The visor, instead of being drawn out to a point, became semiglobular. Numerous holes replaced the mouth-slits (figs. 22 and 30),

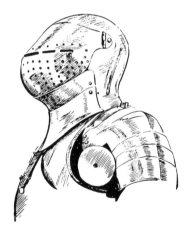

Fig. 29. Great bascinet of Count palatine Frederick the Victorious, about 1450. Made by Tomaso da Missaglia of Milan. (Kunsthistorisches Museum, Vienna.)

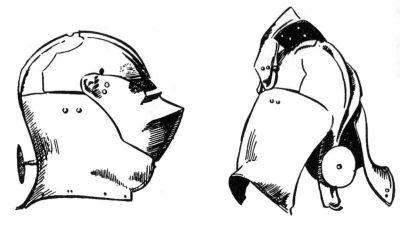

Fig. 30. Armet, Italian about 1474. (a) closed, (b) open and ready to put on.

while the back of the skull, instead of falling in a nearly straight line from the apex to the bottom edge, began to be shaped to the back of the head. Used throughout the fifteenth century, this type of helmet led to the most popular type of sixteenth- and seventeenth-century helmet, known as the "close helmet."

Before then, around 1440, what was once a new style of helmet appeared. Nowadays it is referred to as the "armet," a word that enjoyed a degree of popular use during the fifteenth century. But in the usually vague medieval use of language, the term "armet" seems to have been applied indiscriminately to any sort of visored helmet. Light and close-fitting, the armet provided better protection and more mobility than the bascinet. The drawing (fig. 31) reveals its construction. This style of helmet, developed in Italy, found much favor in France but was not as popular in England. At the same time another helmet type appeared, this time in Germany. There an ancient style had been extremely popular for centuries, a simple iron hat with a broad brim, called a "kettle-hat." In the mid-fifteenth century a much more graceful open helmet, called the "sallet," emerged (fig. 32). Sometimes worn by itself, just as a hat, the sallet often was worn with a separate "bevor" to protect the chin; a coif of mail protected the neck and the back of the head under the tail of the helmet (fig. 32). There were many different forms of sallet used between 1450 and 1510, most of the variations reflecting national fashion.

A feature of these fifteenth-century helmets was the way the top of the skull was drawn out into a keel-like ridge from the brow to the back of the head. In some sallets this ridge became more pronounced and stood up more sharply. In the close helmets of the sixteenth century this feature became even more prominent, some of the later ones standing up like a cock's comb about two inches above the level of the skull.

Fig. 31. Sallet.

While the armet was being developed

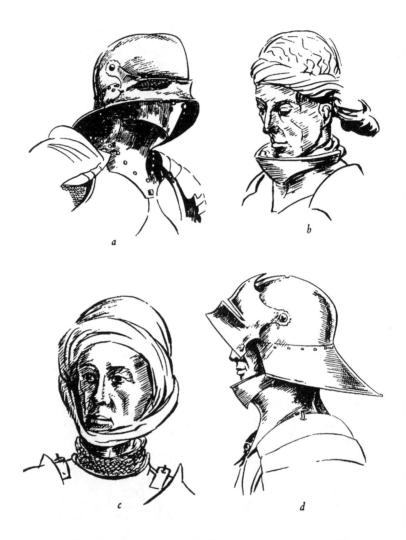

Fig. 32. Sallets in wear: (a) with visor down and bevor up; (b) the long hair done up to go under a sallet; (c) head and chin padded ready for sallet and bevor to go on; (d) sallet with visor raised and falling plate of bevor lowered.

in Italy and the sallet perhaps in Germany, another distinctive form of helmet appeared–or perhaps one should say reappeared–for it was so exactly like certain ancient Greek helmets (the so-called Corinthian type) that it is reasonable to suppose that the

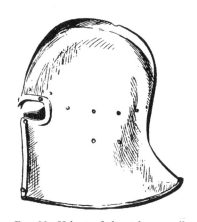

Fig. 33. Helmet of the style generally known today as "Barbute," possibly derived from the ancient Greek Corinthian helmet.

newly kindled interest in Greek statuary and vase-painting had suggested the form to the mid-fifteenth-century Italian armorers. (fig. 33)

Until the second quarter of the seventeenth century, armor was still used in war, though it became more and more unusual to wear a full harness. In an effort to make armor strong enough to withstand the firepower of balls shot from firearms, the harness had become much heavier–in fact, too heavy for practical purposes. No matter how well one built a harness of armor, the development of hand-held firearms and the increasing power of cannon made it virtually impossible to create a completely secure suit of armor. As the sixteenth century wore on, armor was used more and more as "full dress," less and less as

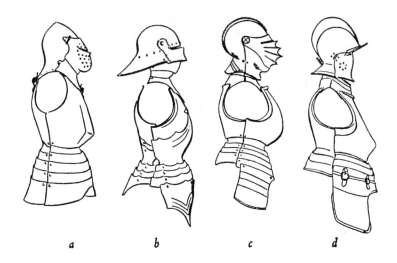

Fig. 34. Cuirass and helmet forms. (a) German, 1430. Great bascinet and "kastenburst." (b) German "Gothic," 1480. Sallet and bevor. (c) "maximilian," 1520. Close helmet with bellows visor. (d) German, 1540. Pointed breastplate and "Burgonet."

"battle-dress." By the end of the century, though plenty of magnificent armor was still being made, its beautiful form had in many respects been lost–for good.

The forms of cuirass and helmet provide the most noticeable characteristics of the armor of this late period of decline. I have already described the basic principles of cuirass design, so I will be brief in glancing at the later types. In the fifteenth century, men-at-arms sometimes went out with only a cuirass and a helmet, dispensing altogether with leg harness, vambraces and pauldrons. This development may

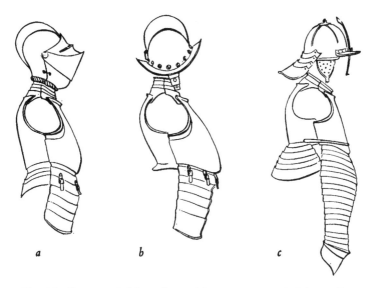

Fig. 35. Cuirass and helmet forms. (a) 1550-1570, with helmet. (b) 1570-1600, with morion. (c) 1620-40, with long tassets and open helmet.

have occurred for purposes of comfort; after 1500 this approach to armor became more common, and many armors were made with extra pieces, such as elongated tassets that protected the thighs, so that part of the armor could be worn. They weren't just commonplace armors either; some surviving ones are indeed very knightly.

The illustrations in Figures 34 and 35 show basic cuirass types between about 1440 and 1650. Most noticeable is the development of the front of the breastplate; from the rounded, globose form of the early sixteenth century, the breastplate began to be drawn out, as it were, around 1535 into a strange-

looking spike-like extension in front. By the 1560's
this look had declined; soon it vanished altogether in
favor of a long breastplate carried right over the
abdomen, with a ridge running down the middle. At
the same time the fauld became smaller, and it
spread out very widely, with its tassets, from the bottom of the breastplate. This change in the fauld
helped to accommodate the large puffed-out "trunk
hose" that had become fashionable. Indeed, armor
closely followed fashion: early in the sixteenth century, when extravagant "puffs and slashes" were popular, armors were actually made in imitation of
puffed and slashed garments. The introduction of the
"peascod" doublet was followed in the 1560's by the
armorers (fig. 35b), and with it the ballooning-out of
the fauld and tassets became more pronounced. With
the end of the Elizabethan period and with the introduction of the so-called "Cavalier" styles of dress,
armor changed again and became hideous (fig. 35c).
(The Elizabethan period, by the way, lasted long
after that redoubtable monarch's death. The period
extends until nearly 1620). The short-waisted doublet
was imitated by a very short, shapeless breastplate;
the fauld became insignificant and carried an enormous pair of very long tassets reaching below the
knees. These tassets of course conformed to the vast,
baggy knee-length breeches that were fashionable
from about 1610 until 1650. These great breeches

had advantages for the marauding soldier, for large quantities of loot could be stuffed into them. The wearing of armor was almost abandoned after 1650, which, if our historical curiosity were to concern simply the look of armor, was a good thing. Better to discard the essential concept of armor than to endure its more horrible styles.

Such was the armor worn by the heavy cavalry in the English Civil War and in the endless wars on the Continent (the Thirty Years War was only one of them). But the big tassets were soon abandoned as the typical trooper wore only "breast and back" and a helmet, sometimes supplemented by a small gorget or a pair of very long cuffed steel gauntlets over a stout leather coat (a "buff coat").

There was a seemingly endless variety of helmets during this period, but all were based on three basic types derived from medieval styles. The close helmet (figs. 34c and 35a) was derived from the great bascinet of the fifteenth century; the burgonet (fig. 34d) was an open-faced helmet with cheek guards developed from the sallet, and various styles of hat-like helmets derived from the old kettle-hat. These last are perhaps the best-known helmets in the entire history of armor—the morion (fig. 35b) and the "cabasset," called by Elizabeth's Englishmen the "Spanish morion" (though the Spaniards rarely used it); it stemmed from a peculiarly Spanish form of fifteenth-century kettle-hat called the cabacete. The well-known "lobster tail" helmet of the English Civil War period was a development of the burgonet (fig. 35c) and lasted until the end of the seventeenth century.

Helm, Shield, and Spurs

TO get a full, accurate picture of the complete harness of armor, we must consider certain accessories, crucial to an understanding of armor and its role in medieval life. These accessories include the helm, shield, sword-belt, and spurs. So we will look at the way helms and shields were made, and at the variations in fashion of sword-belts and spurs.

The medieval helm was often regarded as an extra piece, not an essential part of the complete harness to which belonged the mail coif, or the small nut-shaped helmet and, later, the bascinet, armet, and sallet. Made from several plates of iron riveted together, the helm was a large, somewhat barrel-shaped covering for the head. It began as a simple small helmet, flat-topped, to which a visor had been added to protect the face. The Norse people had

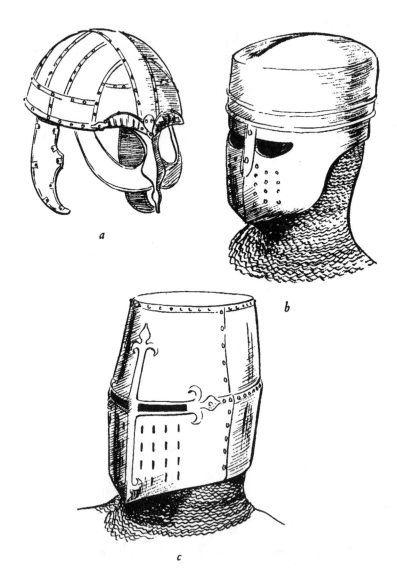

Fig. 36. (a) Visored helmet, Swedish, 7th century. From the grave of a chieftain at Valsgärde. (b) Flat-topped helmet with visor, about 1190. (c) Helm, about 1250.

used a similar visored helmet as early as the seventh century, but it seems to have gone out of favor until the end of the twelfth. By the first years of the thirteenth century it had developed into a complete covering for the head, and was worn as an extra defense over the small iron cap and the mail coif. Figure 36 shows the early visored helmet of about 650 and one of about 1190, and a complete helm of about 1250; figure 37 shows a later development of the helm, circa 1290. Alongside the drawing of this helmet is my depiction of how its five plates were fitted together. This type of helm, with modifications, was used until the early fifteenth century though seldom in war after about 1340; its place was taken by the handier

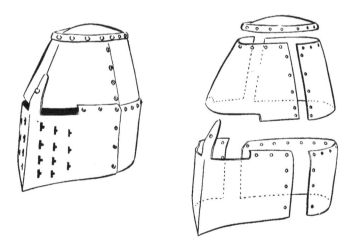

Fig. 37. Helm, about 1290, showing how the five plates are shaped and fitted together.

75

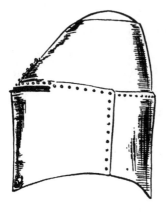

Fig. 38. Helm of the Black Prince (Canterbury Cathedral.)

visored bascinet, and the helm was used in jousts and tournaments. Helms of the late fourteenth and early fifteenth centuries are similar to thirteenth-century ones in construction, but were on the whole a bit heavier, and had rounded tops instead of flat ones. England has some fine examples of these helms–the Black Prince's (1372) in Canterbury Cathedral (fig. 38), Henrv V's (1422) in Westminster Abbey (fig. 39), and two similar ones of the same date in Cobham Church in Kent. These "pot" helms did not rest on the shoulders. Well-designed linings of leather supported them on top of the head, which was covered with the warrior's hair, worn long and bunched up under a small linen cap (called an "arming cap"), the mail coif and sometimes

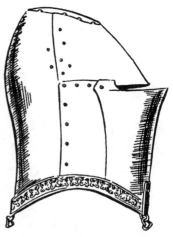

Fig. 39. Helm of Henry V (Westminster Abbey.)

76

a skull-cap of iron.
Only later helms,
those after 1420, rest-
ed on the shoulders,
and these helms were
buckled or bolted to
the chest and back.
Earlier helms were
secured by laces
(leather thongs, proba-
bly), which were fas-
tened to the lining in
front of the ears and
tied at the back of the
head. The last thing

Fig. 40. Helm, possibly of Henry VII
(Westminster Abbey.)

heralds at a tournament used to say before giving the
signal to engage–"laissez aller" ˙ was "lace your
helms."

After about 1420, a special jousting helmet
developed. It was based on the all-purpose type, such
as Henry V's, and, by reason of its shape, has come
to be called the "frog-mouthed" helm. It can be seen
in innumerable pictures and sculptures dating after
1420. There are many examples too; a very fine
(though late) one is in Westminster Abbey, where it
may have been brought at the funeral of Henry VII
in 1509 (fig. 40). These jousting helms were built and
designed on a practical principle: that the thick,

curved front plate, the top of which overlapped the outer rim of the upper plate covering the top of the head, should completely protect the eyes. A warrior still could see clearly through the eye-slit, so long as he hunched his shoulders forward and bent his head, as he would do when charging with a lance. I know this stance enabled the warrior to still see well because I have tried doing so myself with Henry VII's helm in Westminster Abbey. You have to raise your head at the moment when you and your adversary run together. True, at that point you can't see anything, but for the vital moment that is not important. The great thing is that you are fully protected.

From prehistoric times the shield has had many shapes, but its purpose has never changed. In the medieval period the horseman's shield was the most important, though there were other kinds: the small, round "buckler" for fighting on foot, and, in the later part of the Middle Ages, the tall "mantlet" or "pavise" used by archers and cross-bowmen. This tall mantlet was similar to the Roman legionary's long, rectangular concave shield. The earlier form of the knightly shield is aptly described as "kite shaped," but the later smaller ones still tend to be called after objects no longer recognizable—for instance, "heater" shaped. I have never come across a heater shaped like a shield, and I don't expect many readers have either. It is far better to say that the shield of the thirteenth century was shield-shaped: the word itself has come to be used as an adjective denoting the shape. A thing to remember about the difference between real shields of the thirteenth and fourteenth centuries and modern trophy shields or blazerbadges is that the upper edge of the earlier ones never had two concave dips coming to a point in the middle.

The Norsemen sometimes used the kite-shield before the twelfth century, though rarely; theirs was the big round shield, used for fighting on ship or on land. For Norsemen, to fight on land meant to fight on foot; in the rest of Europe, warriors fought in the old Gothic manner—on horseback—and used the kite-shield as early as the ninth century. The kite-shield was used until the mid-twelfth century (the end of the Norman period in English history). After that time, the shield became shorter, and by about 1220 it had become smaller altogether and generally had a straight upper edge—like the shields of the two fighting men in fig. 7.

Shields were always curved around the body, though late in the thirteenth century a perfectly flat and small one was sometimes used. This sort of shield continued right up to the early fifteenth century— Henry V's shield in Westminster Abbey is one of them—though it does not seem to have been so universally used in battle. During the middle years of the fourteenth century a new form appeared, used principally in jousting with the lance. It was in the shape of an irregular rectangle, though please forgive the geometrical impossibility of the expression, and it curved outwards instead of inwards. Some of them had a large notch cut in the upper right-hand corner to serve as a rest to support the couched lance (fig. 41).

Many medieval shields survive, enabling us to study them and thus gain insight into their craftsmanship as we wonder about the battles or one-on-one encounters they withstood. These shields–from the thirteenth, fourteenth, and fifteenth centuries–show quite clearly how they were made. All were made following the same principle: they were made of plywood. The better ones were made of layers of thin boards glued together, with the grain of each layer running at right angles to the one below it. A close-grained wood was used, like beech or linden: in fact, an Old Norse and Saxon expression for a

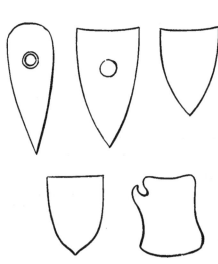

Fig. 41. Shield styles, 1050 - 1450

shield was "the warlinden." This wood was covered on the outside with leather or parchment, which in turn was generally coated with gesso (a prepared surface of plaster as a ground for painting). The surface was painted with the owner's arms or device, sometimes modeled in low relief as well. The shield's insides were covered with textile fabric, sometimes painted linen and sometimes (as with Henry V's) with rich brocade. In the middle of the inner face of the shield was a small rectangular padded cushion sewn into the textile lining and stuffed with tow or horsehair or even hay. This acted as a shock absorber for the forearm.

Various straps, called "enarmes," were fastened to the shield's back; the warrior held the shield with these straps. The ancient shield grip, from the Bronze Age to the Vikings, was a stout bar riveted across the inside of a large hollow boss in the center of the round shield. This boss stuck out in front leaving a deep hollow at the back to accommodate the knuckles. Holding a shield by this means was like holding a dustbin-lid by its handle, except that the shield was flat or curved toward you. The Vikings had an extra support for the arm, a strap toward the left of the shield; a Viking warrior would put his arm through this strap, which made the shield much easier to support and hold. Some extra support may have been used in the Bronze Age too: the Greeks certainly had

it. But, since none of
the wood or leather
backing of the
bronze shields has
survived, which is
what the strap might
have been fixed to,
we cannot be certain
that such support
existed in any signif-
icant, widespread
fashion during the
Bronze Age.

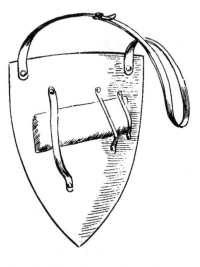

Fig. 42. *The back of a thirteenth-century shield, showing the padded cushion for the arm and the "enarmes" and "Guige" straps.*

The enarmes of
a medieval shield
consisted of three straps. Their placing and arrangement might have varied, but the principle was constant: (1) a strap near the left side, riveted at either
end and set at a slight angle to form a loop wide
enough to take a mailed and muscular forearm; (2) a
similar, shorter strap toward the right edge to take
the wrist and (3) a small strap an inch or two farther
to the right into which the fingers could be slipped if
they were not occupied in holding the reins of a
horse. A further important fitting was a fourth, long
strap called the "guige," by which the shield was
slung around the warrior's neck. (In chronicles and
romances you will often meet with phrases such as

"with his shield on his neck." When you encounter such a phrase, think of the guige and you will understand what the writer means.) This strap, which was actually two straps, like those on a camera case, joined with a buckle and so was adjustable. It was riveted to the shield, one end near each top corner. The rivets for all these straps generally seem to have been put in before the face of the shield was covered and painted (figs. 42 and 43).

You may often see shields of arms sculptured in relief on tombs or on the walls of medieval churches; these are very often shown as if they were hanging by their guide straps from a peg. An especially good example is the series of shields of Henry III's barons displayed on the walls of the choir aisles in Westminster Abbey.

The sword was never fastened directly to a belt girt tightly around the waist. From about 500 BC to AD 900 it was generally carried on a baldric over the shoulder, often with the hilt high up against the chest, but this way was essentially for carrying it for fighting in a chariot or on foot. On horseback the

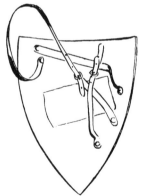

Fig. 43. Another arrangement of straps on a thirteenth century shield.

83

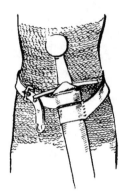

Fig. 44. Method of fastening sword-belt to scabbard in the twelfth century.

warrior needed the hilt lower, especially if he carried a shield, so the man-at-arms of the tenth to the fifteenth centurie's wore his sword-belt slung loosely around his hips or had long "slings" hanging from a waist-belt. Until about 1340, the man-at-arms wore a broad belt fitted in two parts to his scabbard. The belt proper was fastened around the scabbard about six inches below its mouth and then passed over the left hip, around the back, and over the right hip until it met the buckle-flap in front of the body. The buckle-flap was fastened immediately below the scabbard mouth and went across the abdomen toward the right. (This is shown in Figures 44 and 45.) In some parts of Europe—chiefly in England, France, and Spain—these belts were fastened with large buckles. But in Germany, Italy, and Scandinavia they were done more simply: the end of the belt was divided into two tails, and the buckle-flap had no buckle, but two long slits were cut in it. The tails of the belt passed through these slits and were tied in a knot (fig. 45).

With the introduction of the "international" style of plate armor in the third quarter of the fourteenth

Fig. 45. A later belt-fastening of the thirteenth century.

Fig. 46. Belt fastening in the early fourteenth century, where lockets and rings are used instead of wrapping the ends of the belt round the scabbard.

century, a new fashion in sword-belts arrived on the medieval scene. They were no longer slung diagonally across the body, but were worn horizontally low over the hips, with the sword hung at the left side in one of two ways. It was hung either by a hook on the belt that fitted into a ring on the back of the scabbard, or by a pair of little straps on the lower edge of the belt that fastened to buckles on the back of the scabbard. Most belts of this kind seem to have been elaborately made of handsome square or circular plaques of rich goldsmiths' work (figs. 6 and 47), each hinged to its neighbor at the sides.

Early in the fifteenth century—about the time the

Fig. 47. Late fourteenth-century sword-belt of jewelled plaques worn round the hips.

"coat of arms" was dispensed with and the "alwyte" harness of shining steel was worn—the sword was hung from a very narrow belt slung diagonally across the fauld (fig. 48). Later in the century two or more long "sling" straps were suspended from a waistbelt and buckled to or wound around the scabbard, one near its mouth and the other nearly halfway to the point. In this fashion, the scabbard was held at an angle of nearly forty-five degrees to the body, not almost vertically as it had been slung since about 1350.

Fig. 48. Sword-belt worn diagonally across the fauld, 1420-1450.

Fig. 49. An elaboration of the earlier style, 1450-1480.

Fig. 50. Loosely slung sword; and Italian fashion in use between about 1460 and 1510

We cannot discuss armor adequately without mentioning medieval spurs; after all, they played a crucial role not only in how a knight rode his horse but also, by extension, in how he wore armor while riding. There were two kinds of medieval spurs—plain "prick" spurs and rowel spurs, the first being the only kind in use anywhere until about 1270. The Greek and Roman spur was a very small object with a long pyramidal "prick" and very short arms, each ending in a button or rivet to which were fastened straps to hold it around the heel, or perhaps to fix it to a leather boot. Those types of spurs were used in Europe until the seventh or eighth century, after which the arms got much longer, enclosing the whole heel and running along each side of the foot to a point forward of the ankle-bones. At the end of each arm there is a slot, into which are fixed latchets to take the straps that fix the spur by passing under the sole and over the instep. By the end of the twelfth

Fig. 51. Viking spur.

Fig. 52. Twelfth-century spur.

century these arms had become curved, conforming to the shape of the ankle bones (figs. 51 and 52). The strap was then attached to a latchet on the underside of the end of the outer arm. The strap passed under the foot, up through a slot in the end of the inner arm, over the foot, and then through a buckle fixed to the upper side of the end of the outer arm (fig. 53).

The rowel was first used at the end of the thirteenth century. It was small at first, generally with six points, set on the end of a short "neck." By the middle of the fourteenth century, the neck had become longer and the points larger and more numerous; some were like the petals of a daisy, a very popular form of spur having up to 32 points (fig. 54). At the same time the spurs were worn over metal greaves, not mail chausses–the arms

Fig. 53. Early rowel spur, about 1300.

Fig. 54. Spur with large rowel, 1330-1360.

met behind the heel-tendon at a much sharper angle. The neck of the spurs became longer as the fourteenth century wore on. By about 1420 the average length was about four inches, and the points of the rowel were often large. Between about 1415 and 1440–an admittedly short span of time–the arms developed a very deep curve below the anklebones. But after 1440, they reverted again to their old style, though the necks grew longer still, often by the last quarter of the century being eight inches to 10 inches long.

When they see these long spurs and sharp-pointed rowels, many people exclaim, "How awful for the poor horse!" But I believe their sympathy for these long-suffering and long dead animals is needless. These points could not have been driven far into the horse's hide, for they are too closely set for any one point to be able to go in very far: the other points would prevent it. A horse's hide is pretty thick, as well, and by the time the rowel spur was invented most war-horses had textile "bards" or trappers over them which would have mainly prevented the spur from touching the actual hide at all; this may even have been a reason for the use of the rowel, though I think it is unlikely. The extreme length to which the neck grew was a natural result of the development in the fifteenth century of horse armor; the "flanchards" covering the animals' flanks tended to stick out so far that an ordinary short spur wouldn't be able to get anywhere near the horse. In truth, it seems to me, the prick spur, with nothing to stop it from going right in, was a far crueler goad than the most vicious-looking rowel; and the short European prick spur was only a tickler compared with the narrow, two-inch-long spikes of the medieval Arabs' spurs.

Fig. 55.

How Armor Was Worn

NOW that we have had a glimpse of how the knight-ly armor of the Middle Ages was made and how it developed, it seems apt to end with some description of how it was worn. To do so, let's go back to where we came in, with Kunz Schott of Hellingen, Burggraf of Rothenburg, and see how 500 years ago he got into the beautiful armor which is still as fresh and handsome as the last time he got out of it.

In his chamber in Rothenburg Castle, the first thing to catch the eye is the long table set on trestles upon which all the gleaming pieces of armor are laid out, together with sword, spurs, and the short jacket (called a "tabard") which displays Schott's arms, quarterly argent, and gules. Then, imagine that Schott himself comes in, and at once the small, bare room is alive with his vigorous personality. He is

Fig. 56. Arming-cap and scarf round the neck.

burly, quite tall, about thirty-five years old; his hard, rather crafty face is a little repellent, even though he has a bold and merry eye. His odd-looking hair fascinates you: it is long, down to his shoulders, and as he comes in he is stuffing it into a little gaily-embroidered cap like a hairnet. In 1500 it was fashionable to wear the hair long, and the reason was more practical than stylish: when bunched up inside an "arming cap," it made a thick and springy pad all over the head, an excellent shock-absorbing reinforcement for the padded lining of the helmet. Imagine Schott being followed by a young man, one of his followers serving as "Squire of the Body," without whose help Schott wouldn't be able to get into his armor, and whose responsibility it is to keep it cleaned, greased, and properly maintained.

Schott is dressed ready for arming in close-fitting clothes, a long-sleeved tunic reaching to his hips, long hose-like tights, and strong leather shoes. Under the arms of his tunic and at the bend of the elbows are sewn patches of mail, and around the knees of his hose are pads of blanket. He wears, too, a pair of mail breeches, like bathing trunks. Looking at these garments, we are reminded of a fifteenth-century description of "How a man schall be armyd at his ese when he schal fighte on foote." The parts of this description of military underwear apply equally well to fighting on horseback in war. This particular treatise deals with "jousts of peace"; that is, friendly contests in the "lists" or the "champ clos," which is an enclosed space like a boxing-ring in which two contestants fight on foot. It is worth looking at some of this contemporary description of arming, and I shall use the original spelling; it's quite easy to understand, and I think it would be a pity to render it in modern spelling. Here is a part relating to the dress that Schott is wearing:

He schal have noo schirte up on him, but a dowbelet of ffustean lynyd with satene cutte fool of hoolis. [If the spelling here fools you, think of it as ". . . cut full of holes," for ventilation.] The dowbelet muste be strongeli bounde . . . and the gussetis of mayle muste be sowid un to the dowbelet in the boughte of the arm, and under the arme. The armynge poyntis muste be made of fyne twyne such as men make stryngys for crossbowes and they muste be trussid small and poyntid as poyntis. Also they muste be wexid with cordwaineris coode, and then they woll neythir reche nor breke. Also a payre of hosen of stamyn sengall and a peyre of shorte bulwerkis of thynne blanket to put about his knees for chawfynge of his lighernes. Also a peyre of shoon of thickke cordewene....

There also follows some rather obscure and complicated instructions as to how "thre fyne cordis must be faste sowed to the hele of the shoo...." And more to "the midyll of the soole" to lace it up in the manner of football boots, with laces around the foot and around the ankle. The "armynge poyntis" are stout laces made of plaited twine, waxed so that they will neither fray nor break, fastened to the arming doublet on the shoulders and to the hose high up on the outside of the thigh. These "points" are to tie the upper part of the vambrace to the shoulder and secure the top of the cuish.

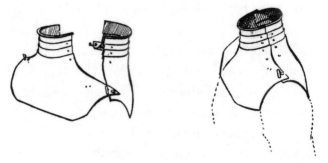

Fig. 57. Schott von Hellingen's gorget.

Fig. 58. His Cuirass.

Schott's man takes the right "lighernes" from the table. The greave is unfastened, so he opens up the two plates on their hinges, and while his master takes hold of the top of the cuish, he clasps the two plates of the greave around the calf of Schott's leg and fastens them on the inside. These greaves are secured by little spring-pins, one at the top and one at the bottom. Fixing the greave automatically places the poleyn in position over the "bulwerkis" (which are pads to prevent the leg harness from chafing at the bend of the knee), so the squire does up the strap that holds it in place. While he is doing this, his master settles the cuish comfortably about his thigh. This is a more complicated piece of armor than the earlier ones of the fourteenth century, for above the main plate are three overlapping plates to extend it upward, in as flexible a way as possible, into the groin and up to the hip. At the top of the main plate is a strong ridge embossed in metal to turn aside the point of any weapon that might run up the leg. To the upper edge of the top plate of the cuish, over the hip, a small flap of leather is riveted; there are two eyelet holes in this flap, and Schott pushes the "armynge poyntis" sewn to his hose through these and ties the "point." This holds the leg harness up and reinforces the fastening of two straps around the thigh that his squire has just buckled. The same procedure is used to protect the left leg. In this armor there are no plated "sabatons"; instead, the only defense for the foot is the stout leather shoe. Next the gorget is put on, covering the neck and upper part of the chest and back, but before putting it on Schott ties a light scarf around his neck to ease the chafing of the steel collars (fig. 56). The gorget is made of two large plates, one at the front and one at the back, and six small overlapping hoops forming three collars fitting one inside the other and bringing the protection right up to the ears. The upper collar has the edge turned over all around to prevent chafing. If you see one of these gorgets closed, you might wonder how it was put on, but the process is really simple; it works in much the same way as the greaves, being pivoted on the left shoulder and secured with a spring catch on the right. The three overlapping collars are also divided in half on each side. So when it is to be put on, the catch is released and the whole thing swings open on the pivot. It is put on over the left shoulder and then is closed around the neck and fastened, and the end of the scarf is pulled out in front.

Once the gorget is properly settled, the "plates"

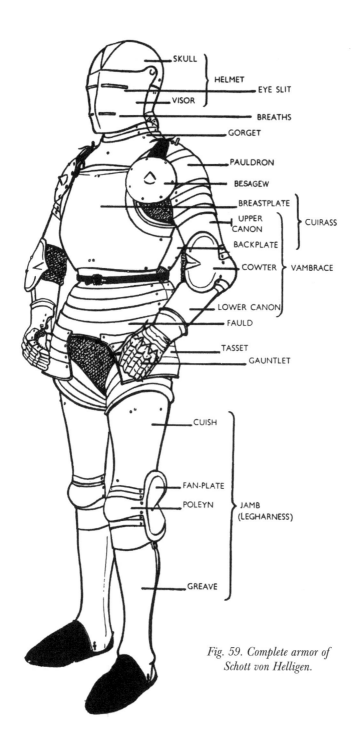

SKULL

HELMET

EYE SLIT

VISOR

BREATHS

GORGET

PAULDRON

BESAGEW

BREASTPLATE

UPPER CANON

BACKPLATE

CUIRASS

COWTER

VAMBRACE

LOWER CANON

FAULD

TASSET

GAUNTLET

CUISH

FAN-PLATE

POLEYN

JAMB (LEGHARNESS)

GREAVE

Fig. 59. Complete armor of Schott von Helligen.

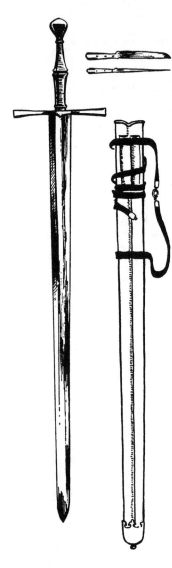

are put on. Schott's cuirass is made in a slightly different way from the earlier ones described in the previous chapter; instead of being hinged on the left side and buckled on the right, the plates are separate, though the fauld and culet are fitted to them in the same way. The breastplate has a narrow movable plate set into each armhole; this gives greater flexibility and more protection than would be the case if the main plate extended farther outward into the armholes.

Schott's squire hands him the breastplate and takes up the backplate himself. The squire puts it into position and holds it in place while his master puts the breastplate on, its rear edges overlapping the front edges of the back-

Fig. 60. His long sword.

plate at his sides, with the rear edges of the fauld plates overlapping the front edges of the culet. While the two of them hold the plates in position, the two straps riveted to the shoulders of the breastplate are secured to the buckles on the shoulders of the back-plate. Last, a narrow strap is fastened tightly around the waist outside both plates. Then the vambraces are put on the arms, following the same method as for the leg harness. The lower canon is snapped shut around the forearm, the couter is settled over the elbow and strapped, and the upper canon goes over the upper arm. Then the small pauldron—more like the light spaudler than the heavy pauldron—is fixed onto the gorget; the arming points on the shoulders of the "dowbelet" are passed through a pair of eyelets on each spaudler and tied.

When this much of the armor is put on, you can see the reason for the "gussetis of mayle" that are sewn to the doublet, for they protect the only bits of the person not covered by plate. The space between the tassets in front is additionally covered, when the warrior has mounted his horse, by the high front of the saddle, and the small discs of steel give extra pro-tection for the armpits that the squire is now fixing to the gorget with arming points. These "besagews" have broad leather straps about six inches long fixed to their backs, and it is through eyelets in the top of the straps that the arming points go, letting the besagews hang free in front of the mailed gaps at the shoulders. With the tying-on of the besagews the main part of the process of arming is finished, but before going any farther the knight moves himself about in all directions to make sure that everything is fitting comfortably, neither too tight nor too loose. He swings his arms, hunches his shoulders, twists his body from side to side, and bends his knees. Everything seems to be in order, so he stoops his head for his squire to put his tabard on over his head. Simply a rectangular piece of velvet with a hole in the middle, the tabard hangs straight down the front and back to a little below the waist. The tabard will be held together by the sword belt.

The squire takes up the long gilt spurs, Schott puts his foot up on a stool, and a spur is buckled to his heel. While his spurs are being put on, he picks up his great sword and pulls it from the scabbard; he wants to make sure that its two edges are as they should be, as sharp (quite literally) as razors. This sword looks pretty heavy; its blade is nearly forty inches long, yet it really is comparatively light, for it weighs a little less than four pounds, and its splendid poise and balance make it feel even lighter. (We often hear tales of how heavy these medieval swords were, that a modern man can scarcely lift them, and so on. This is as non-sensical as the stuff about lifting armored men onto their horses with cranes.) Satisfied with his weapon's

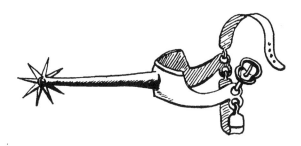

Fig. 61. One of his spurs.

sharpness, Schott puts it back in its scabbard; the squire takes it, unwinds the belt and slings that were wrapped around the scabbard, and buckles it on. Schott is completely armed, except for the gauntlets and helmet he will put on when he is mounted and ready to set out. He picks up his gauntlets and leaves his squire to follow with his helmet, which is one of the later forms of the sallet. The skull is modeled fairly closely to the head, not having the elongated form of many of the German sallets made in the 1480's and 1490's; there are three small plates forming a very short tail to cover the back of the neck. The face opening is large, similar in size to the face of a fourteenth-century bascinet and is covered by a large and deep visor that curves around under the chin. Followed by his squire, Schott strides to the door and down the narrow winding stair. As he goes, you realize his armor doesn't rattle; it is perfectly fitting, making no more noise than a slight rustling and tapping, accompanied by the faint musical chiming of his spurs.

Beyond the dark arch of the doorway the courtyard is shimmering with light and color—light flash-
ing from polished poleyn and cuish, couter, pauldron
and sallet: dazzle of color glowing in heraldic splen-
dor on tabard, pennon, and trapper. About half of
Schott's company are drawn up, sitting on their horses, and ready, only waiting for their leader before
going out on a swift foray into the lands of a neigh-
boring baron. Near the door a groom holds his great
war-horse, called a "destrier," a splendid thorough-
bred a little larger and heavier than a modern hunting horse. While he puts on his gauntlets Schott has
a word with his second in command, Schott's restless
eyes scanning his men as he talks. Then he gets light-
ly into his saddle, settles himself comfortably, and
holds out his hand for his helmet. He takes it, peers
into it for a moment, and clasps it on his head before
fiddling with the lining and his arming cap. He then
buckles the chin-strap and nods to the groom, who
lets go of the horse's head and jumps back as that
proud and highly strung animal tosses his great head,
snorting and dancing and spurning the ground with
his round hoofs in the manner of all horses of blood
and breeding before and since. Then the horse is
away, moving with little dancing steps, only seeming
to be held back from a wild gallop by the masterful
hand of his rider. Just behind Schott rides a young
man of about fourteen, perched high on another

great destrier (Schott's spare mount), and carrying his long lance with its scarlet and white pennon. After him the whole troop, with a brave clatter of hooves and the jingle and clink of arms and harness and much talking and laughter, goes out beneath the echoing arch of the gatehouse and over the draw-bridge, leaving us in the suddenly quiet courtyard with the grooms and the pigeons.

Appendix

SCHOTT VON HELLINGEN

NUREMBERG put a price of 2,000 guilders on the head of Schott von Hellingen, and his period of command is the bloodiest in Nuremberg's history; his troops continuously ambushed Nuremberg soldiers, few of whom escaped with their lives.

Schott's feud with the city had been settled by 1525, and he was given a safe-conduct pass through the city to the Heilsbronner Hof, which, although within the city walls, was the private property of the Markgraf of Ansbach-Bayreuth. Here Schott was attended in his last illness by some of Nuremberg's famous doctors. He died on January 8, 1526. The Hof had its own chapel within its walls, and as late as 1757 a tablet in this chapel was still to be read:

Anno 1526, on Monday after the holy New Year's Day, died the noble and staunch Conrad (Kunz) Schott, Antman of Streitburg, whose soul is now in the care of God.

The castle of Hornburg, for the possession of which Schott defied the Elector Palatine, still exists on the Neckar, with Schott's arms on the lintel of one of the doors. (I must thank Mr. R. T. Gwynn, owner of Schott's armor, for this information and for the opportunity of getting acquainted with the armor itself.)

Bibliography

Blair, Claude. *European Armour.* London, 1958.

Camp. S. J. and Mann, Sir James. *European Arms and Armour.* 3 vols. Wallace Collection Catalogues. London, 1920-45.

Cripps Day, F. H. *Fragmenta Armamentaria.* 6 vols. Privately printed. Frome and London, 1934-56.

Crossley, A. H. *English Church Monuments 1150-1550.* London, 1921.

Dehio, G. and Bezold G. V. *Die Denkmäler der deutschen Bildhauer-kunst.* Vols. I-III. Berlin 1905.

ffoulkes, C. J. *The Armourer and His Craft from the 11th to the 15th Century.* London, 1912.

Fryer, A. C. *Wooden Monumental Effigies.* London, 1924.

Gardner, A. *Alabaster Tombs.* Cambridge, 1940 *Medieval Sculpture in France.* Cambridge, 1931.

Gay, Victor. *Glossaire Archaeologique.* Paris, 1887.

Goldschmidt, A. *Die Skulpturen von Freiburg und Wechselburg.* Berlin, 1924.

Harmand, Adrien, *Jeatane d Arc: Ses Costumes, Son Armure Essai de Reconstruction.* Paris, 1929.

Hewitt, Tohn. *Ancient Armour and Weapons in Europe.* 3 vols. London and Oxford, 1855-60.

Kelly, F. M., and Schwabe, Rudolph. *A Short History of Costume and Armour 1066-1800.* 2 Vols. London, 1931.

Laking, Sir G. F. *A Record of European Armour and Arms through Seven Ages.* 5 vols. London, 1920-22.

Oakeshott, R. Ewart. *The Archaeology of Weapons.* London, 1960.

Prior, E. S., and Gardner, A. *An Account of Medieval Figure Sculpture in England.* Cambridge, 1921.

Thomas, Bruno. *Deutsche Plattnerkunst.* Munich, 1944.

Thomas, B., and Gamber, O. *Die Innsbrucker Plattnerkunst.* Inns-bruck, 1954.

Thordemann, Bengt. *Armour from the Battle of Visby* (English version). Stockholm, 1939.

Trapp, Osward Graf, and Mann, Sir James. *The Armoury of the Castle of Churburg.* London, 1929.

Valencia, Conde de. *Catalogo Historico-descriptivo de la Real Armeria de Madrid.* Madrid, 1898.

Periodicals

The following are the most important periodicals devoted entirely to arms and armor:

American Arms Collector. Towson, Md., 1957- (in progress).

Armes Anciennes. Geneva, 1953- (in progress).

Armi Antichi. Bolletino dell' Academia de S. Marciano, Turin, 1954- (in progress).

Journal of the Arms and Armour Society. London, 1953- (in progress).

Livrustkammaren. Journal of the Royal Armory, Stockholm, 1937- (in progress).

Svenska Vapenhistoriske Arsskrift. Journal of the Swedish Arms and Armour Society, Stockholm (in progress).

Zeitschrift fur Historische Waffen- und Kostdmkunde. Quarterly publication of the now defunct *Verein fur Historische Waffenkunde.* 17 vols. Dresden and Berlin, 1897-1944. (Later revived as the quarterly publication of the Gesellschaft fur Historischc Waffcn- und Kostumkunde. 1959- in progress.)

Glossary

Aketon – part of leather clothes worn under armor, providing protection from the shock of heavy hits to the armored warrior. See gambeson, below.

Alwyte armor – uncovered armor. Also called white armor.

Aventail – a curtain of mail covering the chin and neck and falling like a cape over the shoulders. The English called this covering "aventail." See "camail" (below).

Bannockburn – Scottish village near Stirling. Name of a decisive battle in which Robert the Bruce, King of Scots, defeated England's Edward II in 1314.

Bard – fabric or armor that covered and protected horses.

Bascinet – a spherical-shaped or pointed helmet. Various types of visors often covered the face-opening of these helmets.

Battle of Hastings – fought between Saxon and Norman soldiers in 1066 in a valley north of Hastings in Sussex. William the Conqueror, head of the Normans, triumphed in what has become known to history as the Norman Conquest.

Bayeaux Tapestry – made by women seamstresses, the Bayeaux Tapestry provides a pictorial depiction of scenes leading up to and including the Norman Conquest (see below).

Besagew – a small steel disc protecting an open area in an armor, generally at the elbow or armpit.

Bevor – piece of armor that protects the face and head. It is worn with a helmet. Sometimes spelled "beaver."

Black Prince – Edward Plantagenet, Prince of Wales, a great commander whose military prowess helped the English defeat France at Poitiers in 1356 during the Hundred Years' War.

Buckler – a small, round shield for fighting on foot.

Byrnie – what Nordic people called a mail shirt, a long garment reaching nearly to the knee. Called a hauberk (below) by the remainder of Europe.

Camail – French name for "aventail" (see above).

Champ clos – small enclosure in which duels were fought.

Chausses – tight-fitting armor for the legs and feet, it usually was made of mail.

Closed greaves – metal plates that enclosed, and protected, the legs. One plate was for the front and the other for the back of the leg.

Coat of arms – the name in England for the "jupon" (see below), a garment that covered plates of armor and was usually decorated with the arms of the wearer. After about 1420 in England, this coat of armor was no longer used and the knight appears clad from head to toe in shining steel.

Coat of plates – the name tells the story, for the coat of plates was a sleeveless coat made of small overlapping plates that acted as a defense for the body.

Coif – covering for the head and neck.

Courtrai – city in northwest Belgium.

Couter – plate made to cover the elbow.

Crécy – site of 1346 battle in northern France between the English and the French. England won, thanks mostly to archers and their terrible weapons in the early part of the Hundred Years' War.

Cuirass – The word "cuirass" refers to the whole armor for the body, breast, and back; the term came into use in the fifteenth century and developed from the thirteenth century "cuirie" or "cuiret," which meant a breast defense of (originally) leather.

Cuiret – thirteenth-century term for a leather defense for the breast. See cuirie.

Cuirie – thirteenth-century term meaning a breast defense made of leather. See cuiret.

Demigreaves – light metal greaves occasionally used to protect the front of shins. They were rare until the end of the thirteenth century.

Dupplin Moor – site of 1332 battle in which Scotland suffered a terrible defeat at the hands of the English.

Enarmes – straps fastened to the back of shields.

English Civil War – a series of seventeenth-century battles in the British Isles between Parliamentarians and supporters of the throne.

Fauld – a defense for the abdomen, it consisted of a fabric with iron hoops attached. It was commonplace in the age of armor.

Gambeson – a padded shirt that was worn under armor and acted as a kind of shock absorber that protected the body from the impact of hard-hitting blows. Also called an aketon (see above).

Gamboised cuishes – trouser-like coverings for the thighs.

Gerald of Wales – known as Giraldus Cambrensis,

a twelfth-century chronicler. Gerald's accounts of fighting on the Welsh borders in the late twelfth century provide insight into the weapons and armor of the time. In describing a skirmish between the English and the Welsh, Gerald tells how a Welsh longbowman's arrow was so deadly powerful that it pierced thigh, leather hose, and mail. Such an account helps us understand that, because of advances in weaponry, armor needed to change and improve.

German style – a style of armor that emerged, like the Italian style (see below), after about 1420. One sign of the German fashion is the emergence of the lower part of the breastplate with a rectangular box-like shape that the Germans called "Kastenbrust." Embossed ridges were added later. After about 1440, the box shape was abandoned for elegant, slender armor, with ridges decorating the breastplate. Ridges eventually were added to the rest of the German-style armor.

Gothic armor - name for German armor of the fifteenth century, whose long, slender forms and decorative features slightly resemble Gothic architecture.

Halberd – weapon that resulted from the bill-hook and spear. A halberd essentially had a wide, yet short, blade on a five-foot haft.

Halidon Hill – site of fourteenth-century battle on

the Scottish border. The British won the battle.

Harness – word used to signify armor. When armor was a part of everyday life, it was not called a "suit of armor," but instead simply "an armor" or "harness." The expression "a suit of armor" did not come about until circa 1600.

Hauberk – a long tunic that often extended to the knees; it was made of leather or mail and helped protect the warrior.

Hind tasset – a plate sometimes attached to the backplate; the hind tasset protected the buttocks.

Italian style – a style of armor that emerged after about 1420. Though it resembled the earlier International style, the Italian style tended to be heavier and more robust in appearance.

Jamb – name for the leg harness, armor that protected the legs.

Jupon – coats, sometimes called "gipoun," that were richly decorated with the arms of their wearers and which covered plates of armor. See "coat of arms" (above).

King Edward II – ineffective fourteenth-century English king, he had no skills as a warrior. During his reign, the British suffered terrible losses to the Scots. His barons eventually murdered him.

Kite-shield – apt name describing the shape of an early knightly shield.

Lame – narrow plates fixed to poleyns, armor that provided a defense for knees.

Legionary – member of a Roman army of foot soldiers.

Lisieres d'Arret – another name for stout ribs (see below).

Mail – armor that was flexible, consisting of rings linked together or of small exterior plates.

Mantlet – a tall shield used by archers and crossbowmen. Also called a "pavise."

Muffler – mittens that came at the end of, and thus finished off, many hauberks (see above). The hands slipped through the mufflers, which were made of mail, with a separate place for the thumb.

Norman Conquest – the defeat of Anglo-Saxon England by Norman leader William the Conqueror in 1066.

Piles – arrow-heads.

Poleyns – added in the middle of the thirteenth century to tight-fitting armor for the legs and feet, poleyns were hard defenses for the knees. They were fixed to the bottom of trouser-like coverings for the thighs.

Robert the Bruce – hero to Scottish patriots, he lived from 1274 until 1329. He assumed the Scottish throne at Scone on March 27, 1306.

Sabaton – metal footwear.

Saint George – an early Christian martyr and the patron saint of England. He lived probably in the third century but was not known in England until the eighth.

Sallet – a light helmet that often had a faceguard.

Senlac – the name of the field on which the Battle of Hastings was fought.

Spaudler – series of small overlapping plates that protected the shoulder.

Stout ribs – added to the top of cuishes (see above), stout ribs – or stop ribs – were designed to thwart the point of any weapon that ran along a plate.

Surcoat – A covering for body armor, it once was a flowing nightshirt-like robe of the thirteenth century; then the surcoat became a close-fitting garment, somewhat like a sailor's shirt, fitting closely to the elegant "plates" beneath it.

Tabard – after the jupon (see above) was abandoned, after about 1420, a similar coat of arms became fashionable. This development emerged in the late 1450s, and this loose-hanging coat is called a tabard. By contrast, the jupon was tight-fitting.

Tassets – small plates hanging from the bottom edge of the fauld (see above).

Thirty Years' War – central European war lasting from 1618 until 1648. It started between German Protestants and Catholics but eventually pitted France, Sweden, and Denmark against the Holy Roman Empire and Spain.

Vambrace – armor for the arms. The word "vambrace" once applied only to forearm defense, but by the late fourteenth century the word applied to defense for the whole arm. It covered the entire circumference of the arm.

Warlinden – an Old Norse and Saxon expression for a shield.

White armor – uncovered armor. Also called "alwhyte."

INDEX

Also in the Medieval Knight series
available from Dufour Editions

A Knight and His Castle

Second Edition

EWART OAKESHOTT

Superbly illustrated by the author, he
traces the design, building, and defense of
castles throughout the Middle Ages, and explores
castle armory, daily life, the training of boys
to become knights, sieges, and favorite pastimes
such as hunting and hawking.

*1996, glossary, illustrations, index, 5½ x 8½, 128 pages,
Paper ISBN 0-8023-1294-2*

Also in the Medieval Knight series
available from Dufour Editions

A Knight and His Weapons

Second Edition
EWART OAKESHOTT

Take an engaging journey back in time, when
battles were fought with swords, lances, maces, and
an array of well-crafted devices that could be elegant
and ornate, brutal and efficient, or both. This accessi-
ble, lively, and informative book explores many
facets of the medieval world of weaponry.

1997, glossary, illustrations, index, 5½ x 8½, 128 pages,
Paper ISBN 0-8023-1299-3

Also in the Medieval Knight series
available from Dufour Editions

A Knight in Battle

Second Edition

EWART OAKESHOTT

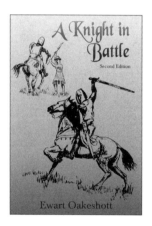

An exciting, informative look at the world
of medieval warfare. Enter an exhilarating time
of change and clashing foes in this highly readable,
authoritative exploration of a dangerous aspect
of medieval life.

1998, glossary, illustrations, index, 5½ x 8½, 144 pages,
Paper ISBN 0-8023-1322-1

Also in the Medieval Knight series
available from Dufour Editions

A Knight and His Horse

Second Edition

EWART OAKESHOTT

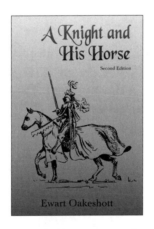

Explore a fascinating dimension of medieval life in
this engaging account of knights and their horses.
Tells how horses were bred and trained for war, and
how they became symbols of social class and sources
of pride. Without a horse, a knight was nothing..

*1999, glossary, illustrations, index, 5½ x 8½, 128 pages,
Paper ISBN 0-8023-1297-7*